Edward Payson Roe

Play and Profit in My Garden

Edward Payson Roe

Play and Profit in My Garden

ISBN/EAN: 9783337068912

Printed in Europe, USA, Canada, Australia, Japan

Cover: Foto ©Lupo / pixelio.de

More available books at **www.hansebooks.com**

IN

MY GARDEN.

BY
REV. E. P. ROE,

AUTHOR OF "BARRIERS BURNED AWAY," "WITHOUT A HOME,"
"NATURE'S SERIAL STORY," ETC.

NEW YORK:
ORANGE JUDD COMPANY,
1899.

Entered, according to Act of Congress, in the year 1886, by the
O. JUDD CO.,
In the Office of the Librarian of Congress, at Washington.

This Book

is

Affectionately Dedicated

to my

Honored Father.

PREFACE TO NEW EDITION.

"Play and Profit in My Garden" was the second book that I wrote, and perhaps into no other have I put so much of my own personality. As I read it now, after the lapse of years, it vividly recalls a period of life that would otherwise have been partially forgotten and indistinct. I wrote it in my early gardening enthusiasm, and much revision might take all the life, freshness and realism from the story, for it is a story of a garden. Manuals have been and will be written by the score, but few actual and truthful garden experiences have been related. There is a difference between a garden sermon and a garden biography. This book is the latter. It gives the ancestry of a garden, its small beginning, growth and maturity. Although the reader may regard it as one of the "short and simple annals of the poor," he may also conclude that if a garden could be made in ground, much of which was so unpromising, there would be a better chance for him with his superior land.

E. P. ROE.

Cornwall-on-the-Hudson, N. Y.,
    May, 1886.

PREFACE.

THIS is not a scientific work, as the reader will soon discover. I know that lofty minds will pass it by in silent disdain. I have not tried to make the world wiser. Let the wise do that.

Nor is it a manual, giving in terse, sharp periods, the greatest amount of accurate information in briefest space. My style, I fear, is like my garden, which grows successfully many weeds, while attempting something useful. I never could write a manual any more than I could work steadily in my garden at one thing all day. I always did like to weed near the strawberry-bed or the raspberries, on the same principle. I fear that when a boy (?) I enjoyed sitting near the choir, where I could glance at the pretty singers during the dry passages of the sermon. Do we not need occasional relaxation from the severe duties of life?

In brief, it is my sincere conviction that a garden is good for humanity (see Genesis ii. 8), and it is my wish to diffuse this belief as widely as possible.

I frankly admit that the following pages are very much the same in character as if I had taken the reader by the arm, from time to time, and strolled around my garden-paths (which are irregular and straggling as my story), and chatted in a familiar way on the topics suggested as we passed along.

I know that I shall be met at the outset by that inevitable Yankee question, "Does a garden pay?"

I might answer indignantly, does it pay to kiss your wife, to dandle your baby, or to go back to the past (?) to look at the choir, or do anything else agreeable to human nature?

Is the gain in health, strength, and happiness, which this Eden form of recreation secures, to be gauged by the dollar symbol?

Can the flavor of your own crisp lettuce or strawberries and cream be bought? Is the perfume of the flowers that your own hands have planted, to be had in the market?

I don't believe that Eden was laid out on the principle of a "truck-garden," every inch being planted in a profitable crop; nor do I think that Adam and Eve bustled out every morning with the expression seen on so many American faces, "Time is money." The question in regard to a garden seems to me to be, shall we enjoy a little bit of Paradise this side of Jordan?

Still aware of the general indifference to Paradise on either side of Jordan, I hasten to state that my garden did pay in dollars and cents, and I think yours can be made to do the same, my reader, as I shall try to prove in the following pages.

CONTENTS.

CHAPTER I.
Will you Walk into my Garden, - • • 7

CHAPTER II.
My Garden Accounted for, - • - - 20

CHAPTER III.
My Garden—Its Location, - • • • 36

CHAPTER IV.
My Garden—How it Grew, - - • - 50

CHAPTER V.
My Garden—What Fruits were Cultivated, - 64

CHAPTER VI.
My Garden—What Fruits were Cultivated, continued, 76

CHAPTER VII.
Markets, • - - - - • - - 94

CHAPTER VIII.
Expenses, • - • - - • - 111

CHAPTER IX.
Ground for a Garden, - • - • - 128

CHAPTER X.
When to Commence a Garden, - - - 146

CONTENTS.

CHAPTER XI.   Page.
We will Go to Work, - - - - - 163

CHAPTER XII.
The Campaign in September, - - - 185

CHAPTER XIII.
Preparing for Winter Quarters, - - - 205

CHAPTER XIV.
Gardening over a Winter Fire, - - - 235

CHAPTER XV.
April, - - - - - - - - 274

CHAPTER XVI.
Grafting or Horticultural Conversion, - - 292

CHAPTER XVII.
Corn and Beans, &c., - - - - - 306

PLAY AND PROFIT

IN

MY GARDEN.

I.

WILL YOU WALK INTO MY GARDEN?

Two thousand dollars seems a snug sum to a quiet, professional man, but to a country parson, pastor of a struggling church, it looms up into the regions of the sublime.

But when at the close of '71 I came to sum up the results of my small garden of about two acres, I found the grand total to be this rather surprising amount.

If this success had grown out of some lucky stroke of fortune, I should not have intruded a small personal matter on the public. But I am one that the fickle goddess has rarely smiled upon, and hard work has been the only Aladdin's lamp of my experience. Again, the world is ever agape at those gifted with genius, who flash with meteoric brilliancy through striking and original means to astonishing results. Alas! my modest little garden has never been the scene of any such agricultural pyrotechnics, and I warn the reader from the start, that he will find nothing to dazzle or bewilder in the following pages. There will be a record of facts and figures, of many blunders, lame experiments, and not a little neglect. In brief, it will be my way of doing it; and already, in imagination, upon the face of many a notable reader, (if I secure the attention of any such,) I see an expression of supreme disgust and horticultural disdain. I hear them say in tones that would blight a hardy perennial:

"The idea of raising anything by such rough commonplace methods; it's a wonder he got his seed back."

Yet, thanks to kindly Mother Earth, she will give a struggling onion or a radish a good lift on in the world, though straggling about in places where they have no business to be, and not planted according to "the book." At times, when absent from home, I have met some of "the agricultural authorities," and have ventured to put my "small treble" in the sonorous discussions of the ways and means. But they would look over their spectacles at me with an expression such as might rest on the venerable faces of a Presbytery of ripe and thoroughly indoctrinated divines, when a young licentiate presumes to express an opinion on that which they had settled long ago. In fact, I was at first led into painful misgivings, and feared that on my return I should find a miserable blight stealing over my garden. It was intimated, as a matter of course, that things wouldn't grow, couldn't grow, ought not to grow, unless it be in an orthodox way, and that with them seemed to mean their way.

But when, fluttering with apprehension, I hastened out among the vegetable heretics, I usually enjoyed the most agreeable surprises. Everything had developed wonderfully in my absence, and plants, that did not seem to grow at all when daily watched, had in the interval, like little tow-headed urchins, not seen for a year or more, taken a palpable step toward robust maturity.

The fact is, vegetables are no respecters of persons, and acknowledge no hereditary, horticultural, or hypercritical rights vested in privileged classes.

Then there is another favored class, who justly boast of their shrewdness. The world finds out that they are smart. That is the word. They have New England "faculty," and do everything by a sort of sleight-of-hand that is almost as surprising as a juggler's marvels. They are as quick and sharp at a bargain as a steel trap. Even while you are gingerly feeling them, and considering the matter in the most circumspect manner, as you think, you are caught before you know it. They are people who do not need capital. They invest their wits, and usually get the Dutchman's "von per shent." Their eyes are natural microscopes, and see chances and openings that are blank walls to ordinary mortals. Now, I have no doubt that there is a scope for this kind of shrewdness in the garden, although Dame Nature is a very matter-of-fact old lady, and not to be imposed upon. Unless her rules and moods are complied with, "we waste our sweetness on the desert air." It is astonishing what credulous humanity can be made to do and believe. One of your smart men can talk and engineer any measure through; but there is just that perverseness about nature, that if a thing is not done exactly right, it is done in vain. If a seed is sown too deeply, or out of season, all the wisdom in the world may settle that it is right, but Nature will prove that it is wrong, and no amount of coaxing or sharp practice will help matters.

But, while highly valuing the keen-eyed thrift that sees diamonds of opportunity in the sands that others plod stolidly over, I must confess that I am not a Yankee. My little ventures have often netted me a handsome loss, and I have again and again seen where I could have made a good round sum when it was a little too late.

In brief, I am a humble disciple of Nature. I sit at her feet and learn. Instead of striding into my garden with a high-sounding theory that a score of savans have sat on, thus giving their seal and sanction, and with this seeking to daunt the good dame, I saunter leisurely around my walks (which much resemble cow-paths), and watch for sly hints, suggestive nods and beckonings. While in this spirit she will often give you a glimpse of a secret, as a kindly old lady shows to her grandchild the end of a paper parcel protruding from her capacious pocket. Follow up sharply and the treasure is yours.

Therefore it has seemed to me that what I have done any one can do, who is willing to soil black clothes and white hands. Of course, there are two other conditions. First, land; second, a love, natural or acquired, for its cultivation. A back-yard in the city can grow little save cats, and the mellowest garden in the world will become a tangle of thorns under a man who hates and shirks its care.

But the love of the soil, like the love of children, is a very general instinct, and though our artificial life is hostile to both, it will be some time yet before the race will betake itself to city boarding-houses, where ground is not and children are forbidden. To that class, who must be ready for the end of the world, since they would bring it about, we have not a word to say.

There is still a most respectable audience among those who continue a little homesick for Eden, and who would gladly go backward and approach somewhat to that state when the first man " was put into the garden to dress and to keep it," and his wife had not meddled with things forbidden.

There are many having land about them like uninvested money, bringing in little or nothing; others for whom it is a bad investment, making for them a yearly loss; still more for whom it is a poor investment, securing but slight and precarious return. Possibly these pages may suggest better things.

There are thousands in cities pining for the pure healthful air of the country. There are multitudes shut up within tenement-houses and brick walls, and paying roundly for their prisons too, where their children grow up pale and sickly, like plants in the shade, poisoned physically and morally by the conditions of their life, who might have a home on some breezy hillside, that would almost, if not more, than pay its own way. But I mean to draw no rose-colored pictures, nor indulge in misleading generalities. By country, I do not mean swamps, or low lands where the mosquitoes keep up the old allopathic treatment, and bleed a man to a skeleton, and then chills and fever step in, and finish him by shaking his bones loose. I mean land with good drainage. Without that, speculators may romance in vain about the healthfulness of the location, such rare salubrity that people do not die, "but dry up and blow away."

Nor do I mean to intimate that any such gardening will answer as was suggested by an enthusiastic Western orator, when he quoted: "Our prairies are so fertile, that we have only to tickle them with a plough and they laugh into a harvest." It took a good deal more than tickling to make my garden produce $2,000 in one summer, I assure you. But I do hope to show some that in their idle, weedy fields, and neglected gardens, there is an unwrought mine of wealth and happiness; and I do mean to prove that what they get will be by the "sweat of the face," as God said of the first gardener when he commenced breaking in such land as ours. (I find the Bible and my garden fit together as accurately as an acorn in its cup, however "the authorities" may disagree.) But before my reader is repelled by this condition, let him ask his physician what he thinks of a good perspiration over the fresh-turned earth. I think that the medical gentleman would be obliged to admit that, like Othello, his occupation would be gone if this corrective and tonic were generally indulged in.

I hope the few preceding paragraphs have not proved a long and tiresome way of saying to the reader "Once upon a time," the brief and classic preface of so many stories. I shall now proceed to tell mine, to faithfully portray my garden as it exists and has existed. I shall carry the reader forward with the season. He shall see the seed planted, and watch it come up and grow into bulky vegetables. My strawberries shall ripen under his eyes, and my vines hang their clusters in aggravating proximity to his nose. And then he shall go to market with them and count the change—and he meantime in his arm-chair. All shall be as clear and graphic as the play wherein Bottom the weaver explained everything, and left little room for the imagination. But, however numerous the defects of the story, it shall be unmarred by one—insincerity. It will be a truthful record of an actual experience. I shall aim to tell simply and naturally how my summer recreation was a source of profit in many ways, for the $2,000 does not sum up all that I gained, by any means. If a little unstrained humor plays over these pages, let it be like the sunlight that falls upon my garden, now lighting up a homely cabbage-patch, now reddening the cheek of the patrician strawberry. If some parts are dull, remember there are dull, dark days in the garden, when the ground is bare and nothing but plodding work to be done. If, now and then, dry spots are found, remember in charity that drought is the worst enemy of gardens as well as books, and if you have seen cherished crops shrivel and wither as I have, you would not be surprised that a few dead leaves mingle with these. If these pages incite a few weary brain-workers to that great duty in our hard-driving American life—healthful recreation; if to some hollow cheeks and still hollower pockets of my beloved brethren of the country pastorate, I can bring a greater fulness by alluring them also into "a garden to dress it and to keep it," I shall have plucked from my little shadow of the lost Eden the choicest fruit of all.

II.

MY GARDEN ACCOUNTED FOR.

ALTHOUGH I do not hold with the late lamented Diedrich Knickerbocker, that in writing a history it is necessary to go back to the pre-Adamic ages and account for everything up to the time in question, still, in presenting my garden to the reader, it is necessary to give some account of myself; for, paradoxical as it may seem, the material garden is largely a mental product. The stony field looks very differently now from what it did when I took it six years ago, and that difference is due mainly to thought. I have planned it before going to sleep at night, and laid it out when mastered by my old enemy, sick headache, and too miserable to think of much else save some favorite hobby. I have plotted it during long, monotonous journeys, and perfected many details before spade or plough touched the heavy loam. It has been almost my only recreation during a country pastorate.

But a deep abiding liking for any pursuit is not the growth of a night. We do not wake up as in the fairy tales and find ourselves or everything around us changed, for it amounts to about the same thing. However general may be the taste for rural life, a most decided predisposition and love of it, as of anything else, must either be inherited or developed by peculiar circumstances. Just those circumstances existed in my early home, and still exist, for the dear old place is in the main unchanged.

The same clear little brook murmurs musically across the lawn and skirts the garden, impeded here and there by water-cresses, and by mimic dams made by other childish hands than mine. The same slumberous sound comes from Moodna Creek as it rolls over the "Tumbling Dam," scene of many thrilling boyish exploits in snaring suckers. On the steep hill behind the house still stand the great chestnut-trees, to which I raced with the turkeys in crisp October dawns, to secure the first downy nuts that the night winds had rattled to the ground. Hard by are yet growing the butternuts that furnished a winter's store to us children and sundry families of red squirrels. In the stony lot the tall pine still breathes its sighs night and day, only they seem more real and mournful than when they fell on my childish ears. The trees in the orchards have lost many of their side-boughs during the storms of past years, but they stand like aged Christian patriarchs, persisting in well-doing though they can no longer bear the fruit of their prime There are the large barn and outbuildings, where we searched for stolen nests with more zest than fortune-hunters for diamonds in the hot African sands. The same grand old trees throw their shadows around the roomy country-house, and even the same white rose-bush climbs to the window of the room of that dear mother, who years ago climbed to where the flowers she so fondly loved do not fade. In the adjoining beds and through the garden still bloom the hardy perennials that her hands planted, and every spring and summer they are her fragrant memorials. Oh, how vividly their perfume brings back her drooping form as she bent over them, and it seems that she has breathed part of her sweet pure spirit into their poor plant life. If we would live pleas-antly in the recollection of those remaining, let not the cold marble in some unvisited graveyard be our only monuments, but plants, trees, and flowers, and then every spring there will be a resurrection of our memory which will continue green and fragrant for months.

My mother was an invalid, but so cheerful a one that she chose the sunniest room of the house as her own, and as boy and youth I never remember entering it without seeing flowers upon her open Bible. From my earliest recollection, she was accustomed to sit in her garden-chair and direct or walk feebly around, and help me in the care of what were to her pets and friends. Oh, that I could help her now with the patience of a man, and atone for the heedlessness and petulance of the boy.

But the one who has done most to inspire me with a fondness and knowledge of gardening, is still at the old homestead—a silver-haired patriarch of eighty-four, and yet "his eye is not dim, nor his natural force abated."

The large square garden with its flower-bordered walks daily prove his skill and vigor;

and though the gardener turns off the heavier work, there are few of its labors he cannot lead off in still. Many a happy hour I have worked there at his side and under his direction. It must be confessed that my experience was not altogether thornless, especially when my task was among the raspberry and blackberry bushes and the day was good for fishing, nor always rose-colored when directed to weed a rose-border. Volumes of poetry have been written about roses, but their bushes in early April are desperately prosaic and inclined to scratch.

Our strawberry-bed also was annually invaded by legions of white clover and sorrel, and my back still aches in memory of the boyish weariness with which I weeded my daily stint. But then, on the other hand, there was a bright side to the picture. I would win gracious smiles from the girls by bringing them a half-bushel of rose-buds on some festival occasion. And even the strawberry-bed, that through much of the year I anathematized by mild boyish expletives, became the scene of a joyous thrill of excitement and exultation, as on the last of May we found the first ripe berry and bore it in triumph to mother. Oh, the wonder she would express. "So early! Why, she thought they were scarcely out of blossom yet. She would get better right away, now that she had strawberries." We were in a mood then to weed strawberry-beds forever.

What saints we would be if we could only keep up our virtuous and exalted states! But I'm afraid I was impatient over and over again before the autumn weeding was complete. I need not descant on the summer and autumn fruits that we indulged in *ad libitum*, nor the luscious melons, revelled in under the shade at noon, and jealously, but often vainly, watched over by night lest the factory urchins should make love to them also. Suffice it to say that taking the sweet with the bitter, as ever must be done in this world, the sweet predominated, and the garden gradually and surely took its place in that warm corner of the heart that we reserve for the things we love.

And even now the sweetest play spell of my middle age is to go back to the old place with its dear memories and associations, and spend a few hours with my honored father in the scene of boyish labors. I usually find him among his flowers and vegetables, armed with his hoe and rake, and it ever seems that he has found in his garden what Adam lost in his—peace and happiness. At the sound of my approaching footsteps he pushes back his broad-brimmed hat and spectacles, and on recognition greets me with a kiss as when I was a little boy, and I am at home.

Sometimes when I am working there with him, it seems as if the mystical and eternal paradise bordered on that old garden, and we might step over into it unawares.

Then after an hour or two of labor follows such a dinner. Benjamin's portion was a morsel compared with the way my plate is heaped, for somehow while there the old boyish appetite comes back, and enough is made way with to make one a very "blue Presbyterian" on any ordinary occasion.

Then comes a stroll to scenes abounding in pleasant memories, or a shady seat in the old garden again.

Truly our Lord called heaven by a sweet alluring name when He said the "Father's house;" and my father's house is to me the best type of the home above.

This then is the good old stock out of which my garden grew. When I remember how my mother, through years of pain and weakness, found sweet solace and unfailing enjoyment in her flowers; when I see my father at an age when to most life is a burden, entering upon the new campaign of the season with all the zest of youth, I feel assured that here is a pleasure that will not satiate and pall upon the taste. And this conviction has been confirmed by much observation. With few exceptions, the mellow and agreeable ladies of my acquaintance are fond of the culture of flowers. When I see a window green with plants, or a porch interlaced with vines and flanked by flower-beds, I am satisfied that there is nothing acid or sharp-set about the lady of the house, and that she sweetens her domestic circle like the lump of sugar that the old Dutch dames suspended over their tables for their guests or family to nibble at while they sipped the then rare beverage of tea. Men whose hobbies are among their trees or gardens seem to grow perennial themselves.

Adjoining my father's place, on what was a barren hillside, stands a noble orchard planted years ago by an old Quaker gentleman, whose memory is still honored in that neighborhood. Some, wise after the fashion of this world, laughed at the gray-headed man as they passed, and shouted from the roadside:

"You will never eat the fruit of those trees, Mr. S——."

"Others will, then," quietly answered the good, benevolent man.

But, bless you, he did eat their fruit year after year, and, for all we know, his life was lengthened out that he might, And others have eaten them too. Not only have three generations of his own family enjoyed them, but a half-dozen families in the vicinity have managed to supply themselves, by hook and by crook, mainly by the former.

He was a kind, genial old gentleman, who had a young heart, and planted better fruit than pippins. It was his delight to visit schools and speak to the young. I can see him now as I remember him when I sat on the front bench among the little boys. His benevolent, placid face was shaded by curling silver locks, and as he stood before us in his plain garb leaning on his gold-headed cane, the rudest and most mischievous urchin was subdued into a sort of sympathetic respect. I think that he will eat some of the fruit of such plantings in heaven.

The worldly-wise are a shallow, short-sighted set after all.

"But what has all this to do with the garden?" growls some critical reader.

Every one of any agricultural experience will tell you that almost all vegetables and fruits are inclined to "sport," digress. Strawberries and string-beans are by no means always logical and consecutive, and as I draw the inspiration of these pages from Nature, lay the blame where it belongs.

But I will immediately step back into the line of succession—the only place for a clergyman, according to the view of some.

Having thus observed that the loving care of a garden, even though it consist of only a cracked teapot, with a struggling plant, such as I have seen under the eaves of a tall tenement-house, is so conducive to health and happiness, and beneficial to character, I determined that whenever opportunity offered, a garden should be a part of my experience. A will usually finds a way, and even during the horror of our civil war, while chaplain at the Fort Monroe hospitals, I had a chance to indulge my bent to some good purpose. The surgeon in charge asked me to assume the care of the hospital farm adjacent to the wards. The patients did the work and renewed their own vigor while supplying the means of health to others. One-armed heroes could sow seed and weed, though they could not dig and hoe. After the usual discouragements in getting started, we made a fine success, and sent fresh vegetables to the patients daily by the four-mule-team load.

After the war, I was settled over a country church, one mile from West Point Military Academy, and of course looked around for a garden as naturally as a migratory water-fowl for water. I know what bird some unsuccessful gardeners will think of, but I will prove them mistaken. The one, I mean the garden not the goose, adjoining the parsonage was little more than a sand heap, and very small. In brief, quite a come-down from my forty-acre rich Virginia farm. There were a vine or two, three cherry-trees, a straggling row of common currants, and five hills of rhubarb. This was my starting point.

That spring I obtained from my late and truly lamented friend, Lindley M. Ferris, Esq., ten dwarf pear-trees, and noble fellows they are proving. From one, last summer, I picked seventy splendid Bartletts.

Then on a bright day, when a steady south breeze was blowing up the river and there was a strong flood-tide, I hired a boat and raised the lid of a large trunk that I was taking home (the old place is home still), and sailed up the Hudson in gallant style, with a craft rigged as one surely never was before.

I soon reached my father's place on Newburgh bay, and there made such a raid as only an old cavalryman can understand. Having loaded my boat with rich and varied spoils of flowers and fruits, I returned, and the results of that expedition are growing more luscious and abundant every year. I had now the nucleus of a garden, and my children could form the associations and acquire the tastes that I had found so pleasant and useful. A sand heap is the place where they are first initiated into its mysteries. Here they plant about everything they can lay their hands on, and often half bury themselves. Innumerable egg-shells have been carefully covered up, in the delusive hope that little chickens would sprout. But have not experienced gardeners sown many high-priced seeds as vainly? Still the credulous little planters are coming on, and this summer the eldest shall have a flower-bed all to herself, with real geraniums and pansies in it, and the very thought will make her eyes sparkle at any time.

I joy to see this budding taste in them and every one, for I believe that the love of the garden here helps prepare us to be with Him in Paradise.

III.

MY GARDEN—ITS LOCATION.

If I could search the country over, I could, perhaps, find few gardens with a finer prospect. It is in the centre of the Switzerland of America—the Highlands of the Hudson; and it slopes nearly to the rocky precipitous bluff overhanging the west shore of the river. On every side there is varied and striking scenery, a happy combination of civilization and the wilderness. Immediately along the river bank are fine cultivated places, the rural homes of people who are surrounded by so much beauty that they may be tempted never to say, with very good grace, "*Nunc dimittas,*" etc. A mile to the northward is that perfection of military posts, West Point, with its smooth, grassy plain, bold shores, and commanding positions bristling with cannon. The stately academic buildings, the substantial quarters with their trim gardens, make all the more inviting a picture when seen against the sombre background where Nature, in her wildest moods, presents the rocky cliff, the black ravine, and shadowy forest.

On the bluff adjoining my garden, Cozzens' great hotel looms up like a mountain of brick. Just beneath, in its cool shadow and almost dashed by the spray of Buttermilk Falls, stands a new hotel, known as the Parry House. Both are patrons of my garden, and are so near that the strawberries hardly stop growing before they are in the mouths of the guests. A little to the north is the village of Highland Falls, my market-town. On the outskirts of this are neat cottages and roomy summer boarding-houses, where city families, at moderate prices, can enjoy mountain air and scenery, while their children are "done brown" by the July sun.

To the west, and just back of the village, rises Bear Mountain and other wooded highlands, abounding in walks, horseback rides, magnificent views, and romantic lakes, that might furnish occupation to the artist and sportsman, and delightful recreation to all not enamored by the richer pleasures of the garden. On the east, within pistol-shot, the Hudson flows grandly by, dotted with white sails, musical with the splashing wheels of passing steamers, and furnishing a broad, cool avenue to my city customers from their hot, dusty streets to the airy summer hotels, where my strawberries, just picked, are ready for their supper.

We have strong, pure mountain air, and

yet are so near the coast, that it is happily tempered by the sea It thus meets the needs of invalids, and probably does them more good than anything else can, save an hour or two daily with a hoe or rake over the fresh soil.

My garden is also a classic region, which is fitting, as gardening is highly classical. I can sit in the shade of my lima beans, or beneath a spreading Kittatinny blackberry bush, eating a juicy berry now and then, as thinking is dry work, and meditate on the past. There before me in the distance rises Fort Putnam, still a stately ruin, and there across the river is the house where Arnold plotted his treason, and there the ravine down which he ran, and the little cove from which he embarked in breathless haste on its discovery. The Father of his country has been here. He may have stood where my garden now is. Hallowed soil! Why should not things grow? Perhaps this accounts for my bush-beans so often aspiring to be climbers. A high and elevating influence still lingers here.

But, after a sultry July day, when the moonlight falls cool and clear on mountain and river, that is the witching time for a stroll in my garden. Then by the weird power of imagination (eating Black-caps in the meantime with the dew on them to keep up the connection with the present) you can conjure up the past. There, on the white ramparts of Fort Putnam, against the northern sky, you can see a shadowy Continental with his matchlock pacing up and down in ghostly vigilance; or the gleaming canvas of the passing vessels on the river can become to you the phantom sails of the British fleet, and the dip of some distant oar that of an emissary of the traitorous Arnold.

If your fancy is of a lighter cast, the fays and sprites of Rodman Drake will light down from

Cro' Nest yonder, and trip a fairy measure on the dewy leaves of the strawberry-bed.

But blare! bang! and the tinkling of fairy music is drowned by the sonorous strains of the hotel band as they tune up for the German. The "fa' o' the fairy feet" will scarcely, we fear, apply to the solid thump of some stately dowager, who now, on her old campaigning-ground, feels the influence that stirred her heart years ago.

The illusion passes, but the Black-caps remain, cool and crisp, and we are comforted.

The guests at the hotel can look down on my garden, and by the aid of a good glass can almost see the berries ripening for their suppers. From little straws on the current I am satisfied that some do look down on the garden in more ways than the one indicated. They are not above its results, and it is astonishing how many berries even the invalids—a large number of the ladies profess to be invalids—can consume, but they regard its care as belonging to the lower and common layers of humanity—in brief, to those who are not rich. Gardeners, like dressmakers, add much to their well-being. They are useful creatures, like cows and other necessary animals. I have had stately beings, whose silks might help maintain their equilibrium, say to me, with a gracious condescending air, "Ah, Mr. Roe, ah, you, ah, raise magnificent strawberries. We enjoy them extremely. Good-evening, sir;" and I am dismissed as the high-born dames who could not read, in olden times waived off, with a passing compliment, some humble poet who had ventured to write a sonnet in their honor. What higher meed could I have than to know that she, robed in a three-hundred-dollar silk, had enjoyed the fruit of my labors "extremely." But I was so oblivious to greatness as to find a check at the hotel-office more satisfactory.

In fact, I have been led to believe that these gilded creatures are not aware of what Horace and Virgil and a host of other very respectable people have said about gardening. Indeed, I am not sure that they are acquainted with the existence of those two worthy gentlemen named. Or they may indulge in the Darwinian theory, and instead of going back to the first gardener for pedigree, hold that they are descended from sundry apes and oysters. From the mental, moral, and physical developments sometimes manifested, I should be at a loss to dispute their claims

But while the above is true of many, the reverse is true of more, and I am fortunate in the location of my garden at a summer resort, for it often brings me in contact with charming people, who have spent much of their money in the culture of heart and brain, and not alone on things that they and their horses must drag around. Who does not despise the man that invariably reminds you of his wealth rather than himself? Who can measure the contempt which that woman inspires who invariably secures attention to her dress, while graces of character are tardily, if ever, discovered. Such big, showy, useless plants are called weeds in the garden.

But there are wealthy people who are the most skilful of alchemists, and refine their money into books, pictures, and intelligent travel, and thence, by a mystic process, into the golden warp and woof of their minds. Modest diamonds may sparkle on their persons, but richer gems drop from their mouths. More truly, they are like the fruits in my garden, that from the gross abundance and materiality at their roots select with delicate precision and exquisite choice that which makes the melting raspberry and luscious grape. Such people do not despise gardening, but rather regard it as a fine art, and a little tasteful present from its products establishes a true freemasonry at once. Thus, in addition to all other uses, your garden teaches you human nature and enriches you with friends.

But how about the prospect when you come to the garden itself? What is the lay of the land? It is a wonder that some of it lays still at all, for it quite approaches a perpendicular. Now, I doubt not but that many of my readers have been imagining a smooth, mellow plot, sloping gently to the south-east, as all orthodox gardens should; they have seen a rich loamy soil that seeds would almost sink into by their own weight. They may have been coveting a sunny, favored spot where the curse, that changed Adam from a gentleman farmer to a hard-working man, is suspended, and the only trouble being to keep things from growing too fast and large. I wish they were right, but the facts are against them.

Nearly half my garden is down hill toward the north, and some of it at an angle that would soon bring one to China, if it continued far enough. Not a little of it is a high, gravelly knoll, on which only certain vegetables that are like the people of Vermont, who get along anywhere, will grow. Therefore, my garden is a sort of agricultural paradox, for though it is mainly down hill, it demands decidedly up-hill work. Still lying between these two northern slopes is a swale of most excellent land, and here I have accomplished my chief successes. My soil has one great advantage. I can get to work on it as soon as the frost is out, and even before. I have put in early crops where the plough or spade turned up frozen lumps of earth that were like small boulders. There is no need of impatient

MY GARDEN—ITS LOCATION.

waiting for the ground to dry out. As a general thing it does that only too fast. In the spring of '71 I had much of my garden made in March, for after heavy rains I can cultivate my knolls when most gardens are in a swampy condition.

But in times of drought, so frequent of late, my ground suffers extremely, and I have had blackberries dry to seeds upon the vines, beets shrivel into little fibrous, leathery knobs, and even the hardy tomato droop and faint, ripening fruit that hardly made a mouthful. The secret of my success lies largely in planting my crops so early that the principal growth is made, and the ground shaded before the drought and heat of summer. Yet, as the soil is new, I find that small fruits, trees, and vines do finely, whenever the season is at all favorable; and if I start early, with liberal stimulus of manure, I can generally make a good crop of vegetables. Still, on my knolls it does not pay to plant such kinds as require a moist, loamy soil, and I have to use all the care and judgment I can to overcome this tendency to excessive dryness. If I could only irrigate my garden I could make it a greater success; but watering by hand is too slow and expensive to pay on a large scale. I tried it pretty thoroughly last summer, but with doubtful success.

One other fact is decidedly in my favor: my garden is so near the river that the air is tempered by the large body of water. In spring and autumn we are exempt from frosts when even a mile or two back they are quite severe. I can thus get my plants started earlier, and enjoy the proceeds of lima beans, tomatoes, etc., later than many near neighbors.

All things considered, it seems to me that, as far as location is concerned, multitudes could start in a position as favorable as my own, and many, in point of ground and exposure, would be much more favorably situated. I acknowledge that one of the chief elements of success is a good market, and of that I will speak in a later chapter. As respects this also, I think that some will be more favorably situated than myself, and some less so.

IV.

MY GARDEN—HOW IT GREW.

A PERSON with a genuine love of gardening is like sorrel, aggressive in his nature. He cannot see a nice piece of ground without mentally plotting it out, and if he gets a chance he is apt to do it in reality. Old King Ahab did a very mean thing even for him, and that is saying a great deal, when he took Naboth's vineyard; but after all it was only a gardener's instinct perverted. It was the most natural thing in the world that he should want the good mellow piece of ground "which was hard by the palace, for a garden of herbs." If woman, who got a gardener in trouble before, had not stepped in, the whole thing might have ended in a fit of sulks, and the greedy old cormorant planted his "yarbs" somewhere else. Not that I mean to run any close parallel between Ahab and myself, or intimate that my agricultural domain was increased by such tragic means as kings and queens have ever been fond of using, but which are not becoming to ordinary people. The process by which my garden expanded from the sandy knoll by the parsonage, would not hurt the conscience of a downy chicken. But the reader can well understand that the latter patch of sand and gravel, mostly in deep shade at that, and the yard that I could nearly jump across, was to me like a cage to a wild bird—a place where it can only flutter, not fly. And yet even this small area, left entirely to my own care, fared sadly. There were busy days when I could touch no garden tool; but just at such times the weeds and grass, my natural enemies, saw their opportunity, it would seem, and made the most of it. Not only would they grow with undaunted vigor through the noonday heat, when my vegetables were wilting, but they made the most rapid night marches. In consequence I would, in a few days, be perfectly aghast, and work beyond my strength to regain lost ground. I found this would not answer; so I employed a worthy German, by name of Breakbill, to supplement my labors, but soon found that his bill would break me, for the provident Teuton naturally reasoned that a job in a small garden, like a small baby, needed much nursing. Unless he used great precaution he would hoe a short row through unprofitably quick. I soon found that at this rate the market would be the cheapest place for vegetables, and those sent from New York were scarcely less wilted than such as I could raise in my hot sand.

But the fire burned and smouldered, and

must break out somewhere. A little incident, about midsummer, added fuel to the flame. I had several strawberries of my own, (I think there were enough to justify the plural number,) during the first season, but after my home experience I naturally wanted a few more. So I made arrangements with a neighboring gardener to supply me. We had a small dish once for supper, and I took some to the sick a few times, and then had my bill. "Seven dollars and a half!" We might as well indulge in rubies by the quart. We all professed that we had lost our taste for strawberries. They are said to contain much iron and to be a great tonic, but those we had seemed impregnated with all the precious metals, and to be very depleting

But I was growing a thought, if not strawberries, and it finally fruited in this resolve: I will have a larger garden and a gardener, and make them pay their own way. Then, while I am writing a sermon or making calls, the pestiferous weeds will not steal a march on me. I will have a rough and ready lieutenant, who will carry on an active campaign unceasingly, with hoe and fork, while I often retire to the shade to provide the strategy. I find that a good deal of strategy is necessary, especially in hot weather.

Now, my Naboth, whose vineyard is hard by the parsonage, was a most worthy old gentleman that has proved a friend indeed. So far from looking upon him with an evil eye, or meditating against him deadly designs, I would gladly give him a lease of life for nine hundred and ninety-nine years. He lives right on the edge of the bluff overhanging the river, and from his front piazza has one of the finest views in America. Between his house and the parsonage lies the coveted field, and gradually my garden has crept across it, till some good souls, prone to see a dark and tragic ending to most events, have intimated that it would finally push my kindly landlord over the bluff into the river. But though I would like two or three more acres to develop my plans and theories, as well as fruits and vegetables, I can yet assure the reader that with the fate of Ahab before my eyes, I am as law-abiding a citizen as any in my parish.

But no tragic means were necessary for the gradual extension of my garden from the shaded knoll described to its present proportions, for my obliging neighbor kindly staked off about half an acre, and that was my garden in '67. Part of this ground was an apple orchard, and in such dense shade that not even currants would mature; but the majority of it had a very good exposure, and has contained some of my best land ever since. When I took it the soil was in a tolerably fair condition for corn and potatoes, but according to Henderson, and I soon found, experience also, in no state for a garden. It was very stony, and all the finer and more valuable vegetables made slow growth upon it. After it was once ploughed and planted I did nothing more with a horse, not having any, but all was handiwork.

From my easy-going, deliberate Teuton I went to the other extreme, and obtained a choleric Dutchman, who was a perfect steam-engine at work. But he was touchy as gunpowder, and I had to walk around my own garden most circumspectly. If he started off rightly he accomplished wonders; but if wrong, there seemed even greater energy; and how to stop him and correct matters without a grand explosion was a knotty and delicate problem. He was not a gardener by profession, but accustomed to work alone at employment devoid of all the little details that now constantly came up. But we jogged along after a fashion till the busy season was over, and then a stout, young boy and myself carried forward operations alone. That summer I sold from my garden three hundred and fifty-five dollars' worth of vegetables and fruit. I will refer to expenses in another chapter, as I scarcely dare speak of them yet. In addition, our table was supplied on a very different scale from the preceding year.

I resolved, however, that I would not be tyrannized over in my own garden, and determined to be autocrat there myself in the future. I was an amateur, and fond of all sorts of experiments and original methods; and even when having my own way would spoil anything, I wanted it spoiled just to suit me, and no words about it. The garden, of all places, is the place of peace, where the true mystical heart's-ease should grow. But there could be no peace in my garden unless I had my own way, and nobody else his—for a garden, like an asparagus shoot, requires but one head, and any kind of a head is better than a set of scraggly branches. I determined to have no professional or gunpowder people in my garden another year, and if there was any " blowing up " to be done, to reserve that privilege to myself.

I made many blunders, and often worked to poor advantage. I planted varieties of vegetables and fruits that were decidedly inferior. In not a few instances I utterly lost crops, and others did not pay a tithe of the expense, but all the while there was a most profitable growth of experience in addition to healthful exercise and much enjoyment. My family were no longer dependent on New York markets.

In the spring of '68 little over half an acre was added to my garden. I can only give a pretty close approximation now, as the old lines of demarcation are obliterated. Early in March the kindly power that presides over gardeners sent me a helper somewhat to my taste—an intelligent Irishman "just over." His sister was one of our "help," and he had a temporary situation near. Changes occurring threw him out of employment, and soon after he was brought to our house in a critical state, from a sudden and severe attack of illness. Of course, simple humanity required that he should be taken care of, and when he got better he commenced doing little things around to show his good-will. He was very grateful, willing to be told, strong and able to work, though knowing next to nothing about the management of a garden. "Here's a man," I thought, "who wil plant lima beans a foot deep, if I tell him to;" and by the time spring fairly opened he was my gardener, and is with me still. But he plants lima beans now half an inch deep without telling, and does not poke them back in the ground when they first appear to pop out, as he was inclined to do at first. He has become one of the solid citizens, with a goodly bank account. The young boy to whom I have referred, also proved a treasure, and stayed with me till the fall of '71.

I cultivated this season about an acre, and my sales rose to seven hundred and sixty-three dollars and thirty-six cents.

It began to dawn on me that fruit paid better than vegetables, and I steadily increased the area given to its cultivation. During that fall I invested about one hundred dollars in raspberry and blackberry plants. If I had waited till the following spring I suppose I could have bought the same plants for thirty dollars.

In the spring of '69 my garden reached its full dimensions of two and a quarter acres. My sales ran up to one thousand three hundred and eighty-two dollars and eighty-four cents. But that these figures may not mislead, I am bound to confess that expenses thus far fully kept pace. I see now that they were larger than they need to have been, but will explain farther on. Much of my ground was very stony, cold, and soddy, and not in sufficiently good heat to produce large crops of anything. I put on great quantities of green and unrotted manure, but as the season proved dry it was almost a detriment, and did not improve the land as it would if the summer had been moist. Many of my crops did not return their cost, and were of a kind that do not pay in such a garden as mine.

I kept setting out fruit, though not nearly as rapidly as I ought. If I had from the first put two-thirds of my ground in strawberries and raspberries, and used my fertilizers on them, instead of sweet corn, peas, and potatoes, my garden would have told a very much better story.

Undaunted by the summing up of the year's results, I went into the campaign of 1870 with renewed zest, hoping to make a wide and favorable margin in the debit and credit sides of my balance-sheet.

But the season proved one of unparalleled drought in our vicinity, while along the coast and about New York showers were abundant. New York vegetables were, therefore, fine, and our own poor. Berries dried upon the vines. Most of my cabbages perished from the club-foot, and the results fell short of what I hoped; and yet, under the circumstances, they were large, due to the fact that my fruit was coming into bearing.

My sales in '70 reached one thousand four hundred and ninety-six dollars and eighty-five cents.

Then dawned '71, in which I had abundant reward. Though my fruit had not made the growth I had hoped on account of the drought, still I had a greater breadth in bearing; the season, all things considered, was much more favorable.

The grand total, Dec. 31, was two thousand and eleven dollars and sixty-nine cents.

V.

MY GARDEN—WHAT FRUITS WERE CULTIVATED.

My readers will naturally suppose that the two and a quarter acres that produced two thousand dollars in one summer are not the bare, stony field I found it; nor would they be mistaken. A more luxuriant plot of ground about June 30th could hardly be found. Everything there is in the strength of its youth or maturity, and the impression of superabundant vitality is given. Raspberries and blackberries toss their forming and ripening fruit high above my head, and the boys picking are utterly lost to view, save where they mount a box to reach the topmost sprays. The bean-poles are no longer gaunt and bare, but slender cones of green. The season is at its height, and the withering breath of hot July has not shrivelled a leaf. At this season you would think there was a great deal in my garden.

In the first place there are sixteen large apple-trees, and though my garden is a grand thing for them, they having improved greatly since the ground has been brought into a high state of cultivation, their shade is mainly lost space. Some of my boys also find more to do under them than where the sun shines. I do not know whether all trees would have the same effect, or whether from the first there has been some mysterious attraction about the apple-tree. Between the fruit on them, though green and bitter in its immaturity, and the shade under them, they have a tempting power that few in my garden resist at all times, while sundry idle urchins, picked up in the streets and put to weeding, are drawn to them with the certainty of gravitation; and the centrifugal force required to keep them out among the vegetables is nearly as exhaustive as doing the weeding one's self. I use the shaded ground however for composts, preparing fruits and vegetables for market, and have lately occupied quite a portion of it as a chicken yard. Though the fruit belongs to my good landlord, he is very generous with it, and I was glad to get the ground with so slight a drawback. But no apples have entered into my sales.

In the next place I had three rows of cherry currants, ninety-three feet long, and one row of forty-eight feet. Besides these there were a number of small plants that have since commenced fruiting, and about twenty-five bushes of the old common kind. Nearly all are young and not very large as yet, and altogether not over ninety are bearing, some producing but

MY GARDEN—WHAT FRUITS WERE CULTIVATED.

a few handfuls. But my journal shows that from this modest plantation of currants four bushels and four quarts were sold during the season, bringing nineteen dollars and thirteen cents. In addition we used not a few ourselves, and some were given away. The most of these bushes were raised from cuttings, the manner of which will be explained farther on. Any one who has enjoyed the cherry-currant with berries two or three times the size of the old common kind, will acknowledge that they are a beautiful and delicious fruit; yet a bush will take up no more room than a full-sized burdock, such as I have seen ornamenting many a back-yard, and occasionally flaunting in front of some shiftless farmer's door; and it will grow about as easily, as we hope to show in the following pages.

Among my currants I have another old-fashioned friend, which, though somewhat soured and thorny in character, nevertheless has its good points, and is well deserving of the limited attention it requires. I refer to the gooseberry, dear to the memory from the innumerable tarts and pies it furnished for our dinner basket in school-days. Its propagation and culture are as simple as those of the currant; so men who are without gooseberries are without excuse. I have twenty-three bushes, and from these two bushels and twenty-two quarts were sold for eleven dollars and sixty-three cents, and sundry quarts disappeared in other ways.

But even these hardy fruits could not stand the severe open winter of '71-2, and the bushes were so much injured that there was but little more than half a crop of currants, and not over half a bushel of gooseberries were picked altogether. Thus the receipts in '72 from the currants fell off ten dollars and forty-one cents from those of the previous season, and the gooseberries scarcely returned anything.

There are fluctuations in the garden as truly as in Wall Street, as the following pages will prove. Only in the garden honest industry is the trait that success crowns in the long run, while in Wall Street, it would seem that a mental "sleight-of-hand" secures the prize.

We next pass on to what some writer calls the "finest fruit God ever made," the strawberry. It is indeed a divine alchemy that can transform clay and water into the luscious Triomphe de Gand, the sprightly Wilson's Seedling, and the aromatic Lenig's White. Little wonder that we look anxiously at our beds in March and April to see how the plants have "wintered." With justifiable solicitude and joy we watch them throwing up their new green foliage in April, and in May becoming such a mass of bloom that it would seem a flurry of snow had passed over the bed. At last, when the June rose, "the queen of flowers," resumes its sweet dominion over our senses, the strawberry stands nearest the throne in Nature's realm.

Passing from the strawberry as a thing of "beauty and a joy forever" (I am sure some varieties will "flourish" in the "New Earth"), to the strawberry as a "crop," may seem to some fair readers a letting down, and yet it is upon the practical phase that I propose to dwell. In '71 I had about five-eighths of an acre in bearing, and from this area sold fifty-seven bushels and two quarts. In addition how many the boys ate in picking, how many my own children devoured in their innumerable raids, how many were given away, I have no means of accurately computing. We also used them like water upon our table, fifteen quarts finding a home market during one day.

Again, the beds were scattered all over the garden, and in looking after this, and strolling around it, I had to pass them continually; and surely the gloomiest ascetic could not resist their alluring red cheeks, as half-hidden, like coy beauties, they peeped out from the partial shade of the leaves. If all eaten during the season in this promiscuous manner were placed in one pile, I fear my friends would regard me with something of the same wonder that Goldsmith's rustics had for their pedagogue's head.

The birds, too, proved arrant thieves. From the sedate robins and demure little wrens to the saucy cedar-birds, with their jaunty red topknots, it was all the same. From the time the berries reddened, like the Great Reformer, they all turned their backs on the "diet of worms," and, though their crops were greatly increased, my crop was sensibly diminished.

But in memory of certain predatory incursions of my own upon strawberry-beds in the past, I felt impelled to charity. I believe, also, that birds and bugs have certain vested rights from Nature that no arbitrary civilization should wrest from them. It is only when they take more than their share that we should commence "proceedings" against them.

But with all these abstractions and without reckoning what was consumed in the miscellaneous ways mentioned, the above-named quantity sold for the good round sum of five hundred and eighty-nine dollars and sixty-five cents.

The next fruit in the order of ripening belongs to the raspberry family, and is familiarly known as the Blackcap. I have cultivated with success three varieties: the Davidson's Thornless, the Mammoth Cluster, and the Doolittle, and find the Doolittles do the most of any of them.

These berries are simply improvements of the wild Blackcap of the woods, and I have seen growing in damp and favored spots as fine fruit as any borne by my cultivated varieties. With those who pride themselves on the pearl of their teeth and the coral of their lips, the Blackcap will never be a favorite; but to us plain people it has been an old friend from the time its purple blood smeared our faces, clothes, and dinner-baskets, and its brambles added largely to the weekly mending.

The Davidson's Thornless is a variety free from sharp spines, and its fruit ripens a week earlier than that of the Doolittle, and therefore is deserving of a place in the garden. The Mammoth Cluster matures the last of all, so that by planting the three varieties named, the season of Blackcaps can be extended almost three times as long as if only one kind were cultivated. This extension could be considerably increased by a judicious selection of soil and exposure. Place the Davidson's Thornless in a warm, sunny spot with a light soil, the Doolittles in the open garden, and the Mammoth Cluster in a cool, moist, and somewhat shaded position, and the canny cultivator has Blackcaps for a month, instead of merely little over a week, by the growth of only one variety.

I had in bearing in '71, one row of the Thornless, one hundred and eighty feet long; three rows of the Doolittles, one hundred and eighty-five feet long; and two rows of the Mammoth Clusters, one hundred and seventy-six feet long; also a row of one hundred feet of the wild Blackcaps of the woods, which I have since dug up and thrown away. There were also some bushes of the Seneca and Miami varieties, which not doing very well with me, shared the same fate. From these seven rows and a few scattered bushes besides, fourteen bushels and twenty-three quarts were sold for the sum of one hundred and eight dollars and forty-seven cents. There was also the same unstinted use of them for preserving and the table in the family, and the same promiscuous filling of mouths at all times and seasons; for who, brought up in the country, could pass a Blackcap bush, purple with fruit, and keep his hands in his **pockets?**

VI.

MY GARDEN—WHAT FRUITS WERE CULTIVATED—CONTINUED.

We next come to the delicate raspberries that melt on your tongue like a snowflake; picked in hot July with the cool morning dew upon them, what could be as refreshing? The old heathen knew enough to cultivate them fourteen centuries ago, while now many a Christian farmer "can't bother with them," and regales his wife and daughters mainly on corn, potatoes, and pork. With very many in the country these delicious small fruits are as neglected as the means of grace. Man is a queer animal to boast of reason; for, go the world over, God's best gifts are generally the most slighted. There is not a farmer but might have a bowl of raspberries and milk for breakfast every day in July. There is not a family controlling twelve square feet of ground but could grace their tea-table with the chief delicacy of the season. People who often make long expeditions through the fields, trampling down their neighbors' grass and grain, to obtain a few quarts of inferior fruit, might have an abundant daily supply within twenty feet of the kitchen-door. The ladies should take the matter of small fruits in hand themselves. With a tithe of the attention they give to their back hair, they could secure from husbands, and those who might become such, quite as much admiration, by placing before the lordly animal a dish that might even tempt a spirit of the air. (Metaphysicians have found the heart and stomach nearer together than the physiologists.) For the encouragement of those who nurse a geranium or monthly rose through the season, it can be stated that a few hills of hardy raspberries would not require half the care.

My plantation consisted of two rows, one hundred and thirteen feet long, of white and red, that by some mistake got mixed when first set out; four rows of White Antwerp, ninety-two feet long; two rows of Clark raspberry, two hundred and twenty feet in length; five rows of the same, of one hundred and eighty-one feet; and one of ninety feet. Of the Philadelphia variety I have three rows of two hundred and twenty feet and two of one hundred and eighty-four feet. In addition, there were four rows of the Franconia, one hundred and twenty-five feet long, and four of the Hudson River Antwerp of the same length. The plants of the two last-named varieties were young, and not in full bearing. There were also quite a large number of scattered bushes of the old purple cane variety, but most of these I had swept away. The fruit is so small, soft, and liable to drop off, that it is scarcely profitable.

From the plants above named I sold thirty-six bushels and nineteen quarts, receiving three hundred and forty-three dollars and eighty-two cents.

In addition to preserving and using them *ad libitum*, as with the other fruits, very many dropped from the vines and were lost. During the height of the season they ripened so rapidly that it seemed impossible to keep up with them; and after some of the intensely hot nights and days in July, every bush would be red with the ripe fruit; and then, before they could be picked in many instances, the ground would be red also, and I usually noticed that the mouths of the pickers were redder still. But I have learned to go on the principle that a boy must get his own basket full before he will zealously begin to fill mine, and this well-established fact must enter into the grower's calculations.

During the year '72, the receipts from the Blackcaps and red raspberries were not kept separate, and I can only give the aggregate of both, which was fifty-four bushels and seven quarts, selling for five hundred and seven dollars, this being a slight advance on the previous year.

The last small fruit of the summer I consider a truly noble one.

If I have a weakness for anything that comes out of the garden, it is the Kittatinny blackberry, when fully ripe. The majority in our cities hardly know the real taste of this fruit for two reasons. First, the berry is black before it is ripe, and is picked a day in advance of its true perfection; and in the second, if it is to be sent any distance, it is too soft in its fully matured state to bear carriage.

"No, sir; I do not like blackberries, with their hard bitter core," said a city lady to me very decidedly. She would hardly like a winter pippin in October. But a Kittatinny or a Lawton blackberry fully ripe will dissolve in one's mouth like so much syllabub; and to the majority it is the most wholesome of fruits.

In our latitude it is very uncertain, being like many people who develop wonderfully under encouraging warmth, but cannot endure coldness.

From the abundance and stockiness of the branching canes you felicitate yourself on the marvellous crop the following season; but when spring comes you may find them hard and dry enough for pea-brush, requiring a double padded buckskin glove to handle them. If they could only be laid down, buried, and thus protected like the raspberry, I think it would pay in some localities; but all the varieties I have seen, except the Wilson, grow as stout and stocky as young oaks, and will bend as easily.

My plantation consisted of three rows of Kittatinny one hundred and fifty feet long, two rows one hundred and seventy-five feet long, and one row of two hundred and fifty-eight feet. I also had two rows of the Lawtons one hundred and sixteen feet long, and five rows of the Wilson variety one hundred and seventy-five feet in length, and a few additional bushes along the garden fence. The vines were young and not in full bearing, and yet my sales amounted to fifteen bushels and twenty-six quarts, realizing one hundred and fifty-two dollars and eight cents. At the same time there was a magnificent growth of canes for bearing in '72, justifying the anticipation of double the crop named. But we had no snow of any consequence in the winter of '71-2, and

March, the most trying month of the year in the garden, was unusually severe and late, so that the vines without any protection nearly all died. Twenty-seven quarts, selling for eight dollars and thirty cents, were the meagre results. In a small garden and for family use it certainly would pay to protect the canes in the winter, and farther on we hope to discuss this matter more fully. With the Wilson variety there would be no great difficulty in doing this, if, as with me, it always grows in a slender, trailing fashion.

The remaining fruit of my garden from which I reaped an income in '71 is the historical and poetical product of the vine—better, I am obliged to confess, in poetry and history, than in reality with me. In our soil and latitude the raising of first-class grapes is a fine art to which I have not attained. And yet I believe it can be done—indeed it has been done, as Mr.

Rickets, of Newburgh, Mr. Ferris, of Poughkeepsie, and others prove annually. And a very small city lot owned by an eminent physician of the first-named town would also make an interesting study to many who require a several-acre sphere in which to develop their incompetency. I should be prejudiced in favor of a doctor who could deal so deftly with Nature, for however it may be in theology, in the garden and sick-room one must not fight her. True skill consists in knowing just how to further and quicken her impulses in accordance with her own moods, or laws, as a philosopher would put it. Perhaps there is scarcely a fruit in which culture makes so great a difference as the grape. Any one can raise vines and leaves, but if you are not careful, they are the main crop.

In no department have I made so many blunders as with my grapes; but if misery loves company, I have plenty of it.

MY GARDEN—WHAT FRUITS WERE CULTIVATED.

The grape-vine is a patient friend, and, therefore, we neglect it. We can train it when convenient after October, so we delay and put it off till spring, and then every cut becomes a bleeding wound. It is nearly hardy, and many varieties will usually endure exposure, so we delay covering till the edge of winter, or risk them above ground altogether. I did this in '71, and scarcely had five pounds of fruit in consequence the next season, when I ought to have had five hundred or a thousand. Then in the spring we can tie them up any time; and in the press of other things and the general spirit of procrastination in which we like to put off everything, even preparing for Paradise till it is almost too late, we leave them till the buds are no longer little hard knobs, but incipient branches that will drop off even if you touch them as one would a baby's cheek. I would like to see the man of superhuman patience who could finish, in an equable frame of mind, the tying up of a long, scraggly vine about the first of May. How the branches twist around and tangle themselves up! How they fall out of hand and strike every possible thing on their way to the ground! How his fingers seem all thumbs, while with many contortions of face in his anxiety and excessive care he tries to tie a lofty spray so as not to knock off a prominent bud, but in the meantime, with his elbows, does the business for a half dozen others unseen! And how at last the ground is sprinkled with little purple germs, each representing two or three clusters that might have ripened in the autumn. Well may he sigh with Whittier, "It might have been!" Premising that the vine was his own, the amateur who could look serene through such an experience would be ready for translation at once, providing he had not neglected his other duties as he had the tying his vines in season.

On some occasions like the above, I am satisfied that the expression on my face might well render sour such grapes as grew on the few buds left.

Then the culture of grapes is one of the most remarkable instances where man's avarice overreaches itself.

"What! cut that splendid branch of new wood way in there?" asks the novice in dismay. "Leave only two or three buds! That seems like throwing away pounds of fruit."

Yes, it "seems;" but your experienced grower cuts as remorselessly as a veteran army surgeon. And yet I am told that professional gardeners are so conscious of this weakness in regard to their own vines, that sometimes they will send for another of the fraternity to do the annual pruning, knowing that the hand of a stranger will be directed by science, unswayed by interest or affection; and in the costly greenhouse it is no trifling matter how the vines are trimmed. (Reflection: I suppose it is on this principle that surgeons and physicians do not like to practise in their own families.)

The great majority of us leave one or more buds too many on every branch, meaning to do some rigorous spring and summer pruning. Where the buds start too thickly we will rub some off, not promiscuously, by late tying, but with great judgment. And when the forming clusters are little furzy blossoms of exquisite perfume, we can go through them on June evenings, and cut out all save the most promising canes. Yes, we can, but do we always in time? Though such a task is the very poetry of gardening, the Eden phase in which we have only o check Nature's too exuberant efforts in our behalf, still the tangled and matted mass of vines and smothered fruit that I have seen in other gardens as well as my own indicate the fatal neglect. In the average garden, procrastination, that we all preach against and nearly all practise, is one of the most common sources o ill-success.

But if a man will study grape-vines and learn grape-vines, he can do some very beautiful things with them, and by attention and outlay can do it on a large scale. Still, as I have said, it is a fine art requiring no little skill, judgment, and thought. A nice balance must be kept between root and vine. You must feed your vine in view of what you wish to produce. It must be pruned with a forethought looking through several summers instead of only one; otherwise you soon have long reaches of barren old wood, with a few clusters at the end, like some dry sermons finishing off with a good practical application.

You must see that those in your employ, economical of time and cord, do not tie them all up in a bunch, as mine once were. On such matters I can give a few crude hints, but when it comes to the niceties of hybridization, etc., such as my medical friend practises in moments of leisure, I have nothing to say.

If any have been beguiled into sitting at my feet as disciples in expectation of the inner mysteries, they had better move on. The oracle is dumb.

In time I hope to raise grapes that "authorities" will press approvingly between their critical lips at a horticultural exhibition. In the meantime I am growing such as people who cannot get better are willing to eat and pay for. My sales in '71 were three hundred and twenty pounds, realizing thirty-seven dollars and ninety-four cents.

It should be added that, though as a family we were not great producers of the classical fruit, we were all great consumers. It seemed also as if the beasts of the field and fowls of the air—things above, on, and under the earth—all conspired to deplete my vines. I do not think over half the crop was sold. It was well that everything and everybody made the most of it, for scarcely a cluster did we get in '72. The vines were not protected, and the severe open winter turned even the Concords into dry sticks. But a good growth was made for '73, and I hope this year to catch up with '71. Some may regard this as crab-like progress.

My pear-trees are young and few, yet in bearing. But the past three seasons we have had some splendid fellows to put away on shelves to ripen for state occasions.

I have quite a number of peach-trees, nearly all natural fruit, that is, grown directly from the pit without the budding in of some approved variety. In '71 a few of the trees commenced bearing, but last year many of them bore finely.

Some of the seedlings produced unusually fine peaches; but partly from neglect and partly from avarice, I permitted them to overbear. Another year I shall believe in the paradox, that when the trees are loaded, if you will pick off two-thirds of the green ones when large as hickory-nuts, you will have more fruit. Moreover, the hornets, wasps, and yellow-jackets got nearly half the crop. As soon as a peach begins to mellow on one cheek they puncture it and appropriate the best part, leaving the remainder to speedy decay. From the time of raspberries forward I hardly know how to deal with these little stern-armed pirates. When you approach they leave you in miserable uncertainty whether they will fight or fly, and most of us would rather endure the stings of conscience than their envenomed attacks. I have hit on one means of fighting them that is doubly "sweet," since it is composed of molasses and water, and gives you "revenge." I fill a smooth china bowl with the liquid and put it under the trees and vines. They get in, but *can't* get out, and, like the "dying swan," they hum themselves to death. Or to indulge in another allusion suitable to their just, but unhappy fate, they die on the same general principle that Mirabeau preferred, when he said, "Intoxicate me with perfume; let me die with the sound of music."

Exit wasp, hornet, yellow-jacket—and my chapter.

VII.

MARKETS.

THE heading of this chapter suggests to the reader a question of no slight importance: "Suppose that I raise all and more than you do, (and there would be no difficulty in doing this,) what shall I do with it?" One of the first things I learned at Sabbath-school was, that it is easier to ask questions than to answer them. I admit at once that this query as to a market must enter into it and modify all garden plans. In the main it is a question which each one who possesses or contemplates a garden must answer for himself. It is one of the points on which judgment, native shrewdness, and especially a knowledge of what is in demand, must be exercised. The merchant would be regarded as very ignorant, to say the least, who should lay in a large stock that he could not sell ; and the agriculturist is equally lacking who plants his land with that for which there is little or no request.

Having learned what is reasonably sure of a prompt sale, judgment must be used in respect to what crops shall be grown, and how much of each ; for there is usually quite a varied choice permitted to the grower.

Again, a little shrewdness in the introduction of a new thing will often create a market.

This is speaking generally. In the following remarks I will try to be as specific as I can, and to give the character of my own market. And yet it is mainly on general principles that one must speak, for this question of a market is so modified by local circumstances, that nothing said of one place will exactly apply to another.

It must be remembered that these articles are written from the stand-point of a professional man, and chiefly for those who propose to make the garden a mere adjunct to some other calling. As my title suggests, I hope to show many who have and many who have not a garden, how they also might find "play and profit" in one.

I will touch but briefly on the great markets of New York and similar large cities. Mr. Henderson, in his well-known book, has clearly presented the nature of vegetable gardening and its rewards. It is shown to be extremely profitable to those who understand it, set about it under the right conditions, and devote their whole energies to it. At the same time, unless one chooses it as a calling, it is a phase of agriculture impossible for a professional man. One must be within three or four miles of the market, and land is so high, competition so keen, that success requires all the skill and energy of the most absorbed and driving business man. In the South a professional man having land near some line of quick transportation north, might often ship vegetables to great advantage. Judging from the price that early produce brings here, it ought to pay them abundantly.

But the fruit market of a large city is a very different affair. This can be supplied from a distance, and generally at a fair profit to the producer. Multitudes are securing a good livelihood in this business, and not a few are amassing fortunes. There is nothing to prevent the merchant or professional man from sharing in these profits. Say one has an acre or more around his country home, and has a little taste and time for gardening. It is no great task to put out fruit-trees and vines; and a Bartlett pear or golden pippin will thrive in some neglected corner where before only weeds were rampant. As we have said, a cherry-currant bush will grow where a burdock may have flourished, and as readily. If one is not artistic and particular as to appearances, he can line his fences with currants and fruit-trees, and leave the open space for strawberries, raspberries, etc. When the owner can give an hour or two a day in supervision and labor, it will go a good way if judiciously expended. In many families there are those who could look after the lighter labors of culture and the preparation of fruit for market. The train or boat takes it to town, and your commission man sells it and makes returns.

The carrying forward of all this on a moderate scale need not require more than a fraction of a man's time, providing he can find suitable assistants; and a sensible man should have no more difficulty in finding these for his garden than for his store or office. The merchant does not give up his store because he has a few incompetent and dishonest clerks; no more should he his garden. In the stocking of his place with fruit, a man must use judgment, not planting whatever he can first lay his hands on, but such kinds as he has found to be in demand, and such as are suitable in their habits of growth to his own locality. Some of his neighbors, no doubt, are raising and selling fruit; let him learn from them the varieties that grow the thriftiest and sell the readiest.

In marketing he should not put good, bad, and indifferent together in any old baskets or boxes that may be lying around, and send it toward the great city, like a man drawing a bow at a venture. Let him go first to the city and find a trustworthy commission-house, (the thing is possible!!) or, at least, let him try several, and selecting the one with whom he is best satisfied, then learn from the market just the kinds of packages that are most approved.

Thus, after some time and trouble in starting, and several dear lessons from experience, there is no doubt that the persisting man might not only supply his own family, but secure a considerable addition to his income. In some respects, I should prefer such a market as I have spoken of to any other; for, while ordinary fruit often sells at very low prices, it always can be sold, and so got off your hands, while superior fruit will invariably bring a good price and often a very large one. Thus your market becomes an incentive to produce the best. Moreover, after your fruit is picked and shipped, you have no more trouble, while a small local market is hopelessly glutted, and you have to make great exertions to prevent parts of crops from perishing on your hands.

But as my experience has been mainly with a local market, I will now restrict my discussion to this phase of the subject.

Under this aspect I would consider the home market, such as a man's own table furnishes, as first in importance. If a family, in ordinarily good circumstances, kept a separate account of the fruit and vegetables bought and used during the year, they would doubtless be surprised at the sum total. But if they could see the amount they could and would consume if they didn't have to buy, surprise would be a very mild way of putting it. A very small piece of ground judiciously cultivated will give a large family a large supply, while acres neglected or poorly managed will yield little save expense and disappointment. Premising that the actual or possible possessor of a little land and his family have a fair average of brains, and are willing to use them in learning how to take care of the garden, just as they would learn to do anything else;—then, if they can regularly give a certain amount of time to its culture, the work can all, or at least mainly, be performed without outside help, and the saving of money expended in the wilted cholera-morbus producing products of the market, the gain, in quality and quantity enjoyed, and in health and pleasure secured, ought to make a sum total that would drive any man with a conscience to the furnishing of his own home supply.

Having done this, and still often possessing a surplus, the grower may very naturally wish to dispose of it. He may be so located as to render it impossible to ship to any large market, or the amount may be too small to make it worth the while. And yet the odd dollars that would be secured if the surplus could find a market, are a consideration.

It must be remembered that all this is not written for those patricians who sell pills and pewter, stocks and justice—in brief, all kinds of merchandise, themselves included sometimes, but who are too proud to dispose of anything from their country-place; nor for those wealthy, easy-going families who consume and give away what they can, and leave the rest to perish, but rather for such as have longings for country-life and garden luxuries, which can only be gratified by careful economy and some financial return; or for those who, having land and needing such return, would only be too glad to know how to secure it. If any professional or business men feel that their "cloth" will not permit them to enter into any negotiations with their grocer or butcher for an exchange for the products of the garden, let them cherish their cloth. We are writing for those whose dignity and reputation do not require such careful nursing.

But through these worthy members of the village commonwealth a local market may soon be discovered and developed. They can in-form the grower what articles are in demand, and by temptingly displaying at these rural centres fruits and vegetables not ordinarily in request, a market can be created for them. Such has been my experience; and perhaps I can best suggest to the reader how to deal with a local market by describing to them my own.

My little plantation is situated on the outskirts of a village of about one thousand five hundred inhabitants. It contains two markets and half a dozen stores, more or less, that keep among their multifarious wares what some of the country-people call "garden sass." Like most places near New York, the supply is derived partly from the surrounding country and partly from Washington Market. When I first commenced, my contributions were small and precarious, but I have since been able to overcrowd our limited market for weeks together with certain articles. Some of the stores daily send a wagon to West Point to accommodate their customers there, and I have had occasional dealings with the West Point market. This enlarges my opportunities somewhat, but beyond the village there was no certainty and regularity of demand. The hotels and boarding-houses I have supplied with little save fruit, and of this phase of my market I will speak later. My gardener has made arrangements with several neighboring families by which he supplies them directly with the best and earliest products at the best retail prices. These swell the aggregate of receipts largely, but when you estimate the time required in obtaining and filling such small orders, and the interruptions they cause in the routine of business, little is gained.

In addition to the regular customers who become dependent on my factotum, Thomas, for part of their daily food, there was a still larger class of "occasionals" who appeared all hours and seasons, with all kinds of vessels and vehicles, at the general salesroom, a wide-spreading apple-tree in the centre of the garden. There was no calculating on this class. Some days they would come in shoals, and on others would not come at all. It seemed that when a cool, crisp head of lettuce presented itself to their fancy, or the thought of relieving the monotony of the day by the sharp biting radish, or aromatic, emotional onion, occurred to them, they immediately seized upon basket and started, and that thus their visits had all the irregularity ever known to belong to human impulses. But Thomas, the head salesman, or Charlie, the book-keeper, was either under the apple-tree, or not far off, and their sudden longings were satisfied

With my limited area of land, Blackcaps and raspberries are the only fruits with which I have been able to overstock the market, even for a brief time. Nor could it be done with these if they would only show a little consideration in ripening. It may be misery to them to be picked, and as "misery loves company," they all aim to meet their fate at once. Some intensely hot day every berry on your bushes will appear ripe. This occurs, too, at the very worst time, just after the Fourth of July, when people, having spent all their money, and satiated themselves with good things, have, in consequence, a little touch of dyspepsia, cholera-morbus, or economical remorse. There is a thinning out at the hotels and boarding-houses, and a general contraction. But in the garden there is a ·general expansion. Berries that were little green knobs in the morning are red and ripe in the evening, and the bushes suddenly become purple and crimson all down the long rows

Indeed, they are like the friends of the rich, who are most prodigal of favors when most unneeded. You can't get them all picked, and such a sudden pressure on a dull village market is apt to "break it down" utterly, as they say in Wall Street.

At times like these Thomas is in a great flutter, and talks "preserves" to his customers with such zeal that you would imagine he was to have an interest in every jar. He knows that those wonderful little combinations of sugar and water that cluster so temptingly on the vines, if not disposed of in a few hours, will disappear and vanish away like the dew of a summer morning, and no trace be left in pocket or day-book. With strawberries I never was able to crowd the market but once, and that was through bad management. On one day we sold ten bushels at the rate of thirty cents per quart, and yet the call for them was not by any means satisfied. Indeed, I think the world's capacity for strawberries has never been fully met; which is to me a proof that the race is not as totally depraved as some imagine. Any fruit containing so much of Eden could scarcely be so universally relished by an utterly fallen race. Some rigid divine may object to this view on the ground that the majority neglect the culture of the strawberry. In reply I would say that they do so on the principle that while all wish to go to heaven, very many seemingly are unwilling to make the effort necessary to get there. I may be illogical as to the race, but as to the strawberry my meaning is clear.

In regard to fruit, my chief markets are the hotels and boarding-houses in the vicinity. To these I probably dispose of four-fifths of my entire crop.

If, from any cause, there are a few hundred

around you who have little to do save digest, it can readily be seen what a market is created. Society is growing refined and wise, putting upon itself many restraints; but it will digest, whether in pain or pleasure. And as a watering-place is one where people come to recruit, that is, eat more than ever before, it is an advantageous locality for a garden.

In closing, therefore, it may be said that the reader contemplating a local market, should, by observation and careful inquiry, learn the nature and extent of the local demand, and first meet this. Then, in addition, he may be able to develop a request for other things that he finds can be raised with profit. But if these hints are not complied with, the sanguine gardener may find at the end of the season that he alone has been **sold.**

VIII.

EXPENSES.

This is rather an ugly chapter to look forward to. If the reader would only permit me to skip this, I am satisfied I could render him desperately in love with gardening, however naturally averse. California, the diamond fields, and Wall Street, would lose all attractions. Men in haste to be rich would only have to start a garden, and then with a pencil figure themselves into a fortune. If the strawberries on five-eighths of an acre sold for five hundred and eighty-nine dollars, what would the strawberries on five acres—fifty acres bring? The result, on paper, almost takes away one's breath.

"Two thousand from two acres!" cries a sanguine reader. "I have twenty acres, and may, therefore, have an income of twenty thousand dollars."

Figure it out on land, my friend, and tell us the result. It evidently is not good for us to grow rich suddenly; there are so few honest ways of doing it, and gardening certainly is not one of them. It is time, perhaps, that this chapter on expenses should be put in as ballast. One can build chateaux en Espagne at little cost over a winter fire, but he cannot put up a summer tool-house without a formidable bill.

Moreover, amateur and inexperienced gardeners are proverbially extravagant, and I have proved no exception. In commencing, our dealings are with a shrewd, practical class, who detect greenness at a glance, and often profit by it. Such worthy souls, doubtless, satisfy their consciences by the thought that they are selling us experience at the same time. The beginner also knows nothing of the short cuts and sleight-of-hand by which a professional often accomplishes wonders. I do not mean tricky practices (Nature will not put up with these), but those skilful touches which a gardener's genius devises; and, let me assure you, there is as much scope for genius and skill in the garden as elsewhere. Many a man who can write an epic cannot raise strawberries, and taking the average of epics, I think he who can do the latter is the more to be commended and honored. But as I went into gardening without genius, skill, or any great experience, I lifted by the main strength of money a great deal more than was necessary, as the following figures will show.

Moreover, I was able to bestow little over an hour a day on the garden. If I had given all my time and thought, I could have saved on every side.

During the four years previous I had merely

made the garden pay its way, selling enough annually to refund the cost of cultivation. In addition, I had an abundant supply for my own family, and this I regarded as my profit. Each year, if we had bought at village prices all that we used, it would have cost us not far from five hundred dollars. In brief, we could have afforded no such supply. But when you go to market among the dewy vegetable beds and vines of your own garden, you return with your basket full.

But in '71, after a larger expenditure than will ever be required again on the same ground, there was a very nice margin in cash, as well as a prodigal supply of the home-market.

The first item of expense to which I will direct attention is that for fertilizers. There is not the shadow of a chance for success unless the ground is thoroughly enriched and kept so. Here is where the majority fail. A man might almost as well draw a check on a bank in which he has made no deposit, as to plant seed and fruit in poor ground. Yet multitudes are doing the latter every year and growling over the result. Nature is very independent, and keeps on the even tenor of her way with a sublime indifference to those who disregard her laws. It should be remembered also that land in very fair condition for farm-crops is in no state for a garden. The soil must be deepened and thoroughly warmed and mellowed by manure. During the first year that my garden reached its present limits, I expended not far from four hundred dollars, in this way; and in '71 I laid out sixty-eight dollars and fifty cents in maintaining the necessary degree of fertility. This was not at all extravagant, for Mr. Henderson (certainly an indisputable authority on such subjects) states that the market-gardens around New York require from fifty to one hundred tons of barnyard manure annually; or if concentrated fertilizers, such as bone-dust, guano, etc., are used, they should be harrowed in at the rate of twelve hundred to two thousand pounds to the acre. But while this is true of land from which two or three crops of vegetables are taken during the season, it is also true that many kinds of fruit would not bear such high stimulating. It seems to me that my Clark and Philadelphia raspberry and the blackberry vines would grow like "Jack's bean" under such treatment. As it is, they are prone to make too large a growth. But Antwerps, strawberries, and most vegetables require high feeding, and every year the cost of enriching the ground must be considerable. In our vicinity also we have to pay a good round sum for manure—the prices varying from two dollars to two and a half per load, and I have paid as high as three dollars. For loads I must take what is brought, and they have varied in weight from five hundred to two thousand pounds. At first not a few of strawy stuff were delivered which, when well decayed, the neighbors said might make a wheelbarrow full of manure. But we have learned wisdom, and such loads are now taken to some other market. Thomas keeps a sharp eye out and often pounces down on a quantity that has good solid weight and substance.

I would advise the reader to economize in every possible way, but not to carry it too far in the enriching of his ground. If he keeps domestic animals, and will gather a large quantity of leaves every fall, mingling with these the refuse of the house, he can soon have what is justly termed the "farmer's bank" at home No gardener can prosper whose crops grow weak and spindling from poverty of soil.

My next, and by far the largest item of expense, was for labor. I now see that it was much too large. Last year I reduced it considerably, and hope to lessen it still more the coming season. This expense has been nearly doubled from the fact that I could not use the plough in my garden, and that my entire two acres and a quarter had to be dug over and cultivated by hand. During the present season I mean to introduce the plough wherever possible. Heretofore, not having a horse, and often being unable to obtain one suitable, I resolved to be independent and put on a force that could do everything with the fork and hoe. Moreover, in the gradual growth of my garden, and under the peculiar management of an amateur, things have been planted crosswise and sidewise, and so mixed up generally that it was hard to cultivate one crop with a horse without damaging another. But I have learned to realize that, apart from the great saving of expense, there is nothing equal to a plough for the thorough deepening and pulverization of the soil. It is almost impossible to dig ground full of cobble-stones, as mine is, sufficiently deep, and it is wholly so to find a man who will do it. But the first dry spell of summer will show you the folly of shallow cultivation.

Thomas stays with me throughout the year, and his wages in '71 amounted to two hundred and eighty-nine dollars and twenty-four cents. It is true that I could dispense with his services three months out of the year, but it would be very poor policy to lose a good gardener to make this small saving. Charlie, who kept the books, looked after the sales, picking of fruit, etc., was with me that season five months and a half, and he was paid one hundred and forty-eight dollars and fifty cents. I also engaged a general assistant at one dollar and fifty cents per day, and one hundred and fifty-four dollars and forty-five cents sum up his receipts. In addition, extra labor was employed to the amount of one hundred and eighty-two dollars and sixty-seven cents during the summer. In the berry season boys picked the fruit at one and one-half cents per quart, and thirty-four dollars and seven cents was the total of their earnings. I also paid ten dollars and thirty-nine cents for the use of a team, and seven dollars and twenty-five cents in an attempt to water my strawberry-beds on a large scale during a very serious drought in May. I am not sure but I did as much harm as good, but of this more anon. I estimate the board of help at three hundred and seventeen dollars and fifty cents, and thus the total of my labor bill amounts to one thousand one hundred and thirty-eight dollars and seven cents.

Now I am satisfied that if I could have given more time and thought to the garden, and if its heavier labors could have been performed with a plough, at least four hundred dollars could have been saved from this amount. I would also add that the bulk of this labor was expended on the vegetables that with me make nothing like so large a return as fruit. Even where the latter is cultivated by hand only, it does not seem with me to require anything like the labor of a vegetable garden. The strawberries are the most exacting, but if they were kept rigidly in rows they could be managed with comparatively small outlay, and raspberries so shade the ground that weeds have but little chance. Every kind of fruit can be so planted that a plough running between them will leave little for hand work, and therefore my labor bill is not so discouraging as at first it might seem.

I write with the expectation that the majority will greatly improve on my experience. Many may not have as good a market as I have had, but by more economical cultivation they can secure as favorable a margin of profit.

Then my seed bill was no bagatelle. I have a weakness for seeds, and every year buy many more than are needful. They are such suggestive things, so full of promise, but, also, like many things in this world, so often bringing disappointment. You sometimes find yourself like certain moral reformers who are apparently sowing considerable good seed, which comes up only as weeds; or like some short-sighted philosophers who scatter theories that produce a very different crop from what they expected. When you plant a thought or a seed you cannot be perfectly sure what it will develop into. But after dealing with R. H. Allen & Co., New York, for about nine years, I find that the prospect of vegetable heretics is very small, and that they never try to improve their seed on the principle of old wine. And when I receive one of Mr. Vick's dainty packages of flower-seeds, I have not so much faith and hope as knowledge of the results. This being true, how can one look over their tempting catalogues and deny himself the innumerable good dinners suggested, or forbear the chance of robbing life of its monotony by surrounding one's path by all the colors of the rainbow. Mr. Vick can insure that every breeze through your open windows shall be like the "gales of Araby the blest."

Going into a seed store is like a ramble through Dodd & Mead's, Randolph's, or Scribner's. The books you take up are so suggestive of good things and good times. You know you cannot read them all, but you look around as the gourmand gloats over a sumptuous feast, devouring with his eyes that which he sighingly acknowledges as far too much for his capacity. So the sample boxes and bins of seeds have for the amateur gardener a strange fascination. He stands over and daintily fingers them; compares one variety with another, wondering at the endless differences. Then comes the temptation to let Nature develop the diversity still more clearly in a little serial story, of which every spring and summer morning will give you a new chapter. Invite your customers to your stores, and they will double their orders!

But this does not pay in the market-garden, when you are seeking to raise what will yield and sell the best; and the practical man behind the counter, knowing your purpose, will say significantly, "That is what you want," pointing to some standard variety not half so expensive or promising as others that may have taken your eye. It is a good deal with seeds as people, the most showy and taking at first sight are not the best. In both cases the most showy are the most costly. But I never could resist the "novelties," though some of them turned out to be old acquaintances dressed up in new names, and more of them prove like many of the distingué people one meets at a watering-place who will not bear investigation. Still I expect I shall go on buying costly novelties to the end of life. There is an innate passion for speculation in human nature, and this is perhaps so mild a form of its indulgence as to be permissible to a minister.

Then it is well to sow seed thickly, as it must run a gauntlet of late frosts, drought, cold rains, and bugs innumerable, and it is much more profitable to thin out than plant over again. My seed bill was fifty-one dollars and thirty-five cents, but I am satisfied that thirty dollars would have bought all necessary.

For tools thirty-seven dollars and ninety-five cents were expended, but three-fourths of this sum went for a large water-barrel on wheels which saves the labor of carrying it by hand to the hot-beds and cold frames. Three dollars was expended for glass, and seventeen dollars and fifty cents for one thousand raspberry stakes, and forty-one dollars and twenty-one cents for crates and berry-baskets. My flowers cost me eight dollars and ninety-five cents, and this was the best investment made, though the returns do not appear on the cash account. Miscellaneous items amount to fifteen dollars and six cents, and I paid one hundred dollars rent for the land. Summing up all these items of expense, we have a total of one thousand four hundred and eighty-one dollars and fifty-nine cents.

I also allowed the village merchants fifteen per cent. on the retail price when they sold for me on commission, and this was not always deducted when the sales were entered on the day-book. Some losses occurred, also, through articles becoming stale and unsalable, and by arrangement, were charged to me in settlement. These, with the commission, I have liberally estimated at seventy-six dollars and thirty cents, which, added to the above amount, makes the entire expense of the season one thousand five hundred and fifty-seven dollars and eighty-nine cents, leaving four hundred and fifty-three dollars and eighty cents as a margin of profit.

In addition, there was a most abundant home supply of all the good things of the garden throughout the year, and in view of this I sum up my profits for '71 at one thousand dollars.

IX.

GROUND FOR A GARDEN—WHAT KIND SHALL I TAKE.

We would say in general, the best you can get, adding, any that you can get rather than not have a garden at all. Plants like to grow and Nature likes to have them. The most unpromising spots have been made quite Eden-like, and there is a principle in our nature that leads us to enjoy conquering and subduing. The civilized state of our society prevents our doing this on the Cæsar and Alexander plan, and that phase which modern belles often push to such extremes, is scarcely a manly recreation. But the subduing of a wild stony piece of land still affords true scope for masculine energy, and surely there is a keen satisfaction in taking a rough field, a tangled thorny thicket, a jumble of rocks and stumps, and by the dint of honest toil, like a hard-fought battle, changing all into smooth, yielding fertility.

I fear most of my readers are saying that it would be a greater satisfaction to find such a smooth piece of ground to begin with. Well, that is not unwise, considering that the subduing process is a very expensive luxury. But remember that even smooth land with an inviting surface is not always the best. There is just as much difference in the character of ground as in that of people, and before entering into intimate relations with either, some little investigation is necessary. It is said of some persons that the more you do for them the worse they treat you. There is the same grain of truth in this remark when applied to certain kinds of land. There are soils justly termed "hungry, ungrateful." It is next to impossible to make them rich, still more so to keep them fertile. Manure goes through them like a sieve, or money through a spendthrift's hands. Enrich it as you please one season, you get little advantage from the outlay the following. That which should have given you fatness year after year, has vanished, washed down by the rains out of sight. It may benefit land in China, but has little effect here. And yet this sandy, gravelly ground, with a leachy subsoil, is very abundant on our Atlantic coast, and in many districts we can find no other. It must be dealt with after its own character. We would advise the reader to shun such land if possible, but if the fates decree that he should cultivate land with a little more of the curse on it than some other, the following hints may be of use. If the soil is not utterly porous and leachy, it may be somewhat permanently improved by the ploughing in of green crops, as clover or buckwheat. If clay can be obtained at no great distance, and at moderate cost, it might pay well on a small scale to topdress the garden thoroughly and often, with this, thus giving the soil a greater consistency and retaining power. Mr. Thomas Skene, the accomplished gardener on Gov. Fish's estate, which is just across the river from us, described to me a very successful experiment in the use of clay. In the grounds under his care, there was a steep hill-side facing the south-east. It was so dry, leachy, and barren, that nothing would grow, and it was impossible to keep a pretty green sod on the place. The loose sand and gravel would not retain manure long enough for any real benefit. Mr. Skene remedied the evil in the following simple way: Commencing at the bottom of the hill, he had his men cut a trench two feet deep, and in this he put in about six inches of clay. Then a strip of soil on the upper side of this trench was thrown into it, thus leaving another trench, side by side, and of the same depth of the first; and clay was put in this also. Thus the whole hill-side was regularly trenched over, and an artificial clay subsoil that would hold water and prevent manure from leaching away, put under the dry barren place. The result was most favorable; the grass no longer dies out, but remains green and growing throughout the summer. But in the main such land is dealt with as we do with the shiftless poor, giving a little at a time, and making it go as far as possible. In the first place, the manures used should contain much vegetable matter, and not be light and heating in their character. That from the cow stable is specially valuable. Decayed leaves, sods, and muck sweetened and pulverized by the action of frost, are all excellent. Horse manure mixed with these ingredients is far better than if used alone. In either case, the fertilizer should be thoroughly rotted, so that the plants can use it at once. This result can be secured by preparing the manure one year for the next. The heap should be cut down and turned two or three times during the season, and if the pile consists only of stable manure, much oftener to prevent its heating and burning, and if possible, the process should be carried forward under shelter from the sun and rain. Thus the mass becomes well decayed, pulverized, and with no heating properties, and so can be directly applied in the hill or row with the seed or around the plant. In this way you outgeneral the leachy soil, for the manure concentrated immediately around the plant so stimulates it that its growth is made, and the crop secured before the spring and summer rains can wash the fertilizers away.

Such land is also greatly improved by mulching, that is, by a covering of coarse litter, leaves, etc. This keeps the surface moist, shields from the special enemy of such a soil, drouth, and by its gradual decay keeps up a certain degree of fertility. Even when using manure broadcast on such land, I have found it better to apply it to the surface, for then it takes longer to wash through out of sight and use.

Ground of this character has one great advantage—it is usually quicker, earlier than any other, which is, for a market garden, a most important consideration. The moment the frost is out you can work it, put in your seed, and no amount of wet weather can prevent the cultivation of the crops. While some neignbor may be looking helplessly at his wet clay or heavy loam, you are driving spring operations with Napoleonic energy. But if there comes a drouth in June or July, your crops may be standing still or going back, while your neighbor's are growing luxuriantly. Still, the probabilities are, that you will always be earliest in the market, and can chuckle over the first green peas of the season, though your crops will not be so heavy as those on your neighbor's slower but surer ground.

The next soil of which I shall speak is just the opposite in character, and not much if at all better—a heavy, adhesive clay, and a subsoil that will hold water like india rubber. What shall we do with this? Let it alone if you can find any better. But if here again fate is against you, and such ground must be cultivated or none at all, then here, also, skill and industry can wring from reluctant Nature a fair return. This sour, cold, unyielding soil, like a churlish disposition, can be greatly improved by kindly treatment. It wants mellowing up as so many people do. Though in both cases we like to go into the improving business where it can be done readily, and effort goes a good ways; still, when driven to it by conscience or necessity, we find much improvement possible, even under the most adverse circumstances.

In no instance is the old adage more clearly verified, "Too much of a good thing," etc., as with the soil in question. Water, moisture, is the prime necessity of the garden, but this kind of land retains it to such a degree that there is always too much on hand. In the heat of summer the ground is like a sun-dried brick, while its roots are mouldering in a sour, soggy soil. The first step is to drain off the evil. Too much water in land is like selfishness in character. There is no chance for real improvement till selfishness is reduced to a judicial regard for self-interest; and the land that persists in holding water, instead of giving it to the air above and springs below, is past praying for. Draining is a prime necessity, and the owner must set about it at once, unless he would have his garden a scene of disappointment and almost wasted labor. If there are stones on the land, in no better way can he dispose of them than in the formation of drains. If the garden so slopes that one drain, five or six feet deep, can be cut through near the centre, all the better. If the soil is very stiff and wet, then side drains, fifteen feet apart, and three and a half feet deep, should be dug, leading into the main ditch; but if the subsoil is so porous as to give the water some chance to get through then these laterals can be cut twenty-five feet apart. The nearness and number of drains is a question of judgment that must be decided on the ground; and if the owner has had no experience, it would be wise to call in a few neighbors. Strike an average between their advice, and you will probably hit on the right course. Or, what would be still more to the point, if you could find one practical man, who has successfully and economically done the work, you had better follow his example.

If there are cobble-stones on your land, then the common rubber drain will answer. Throw them into the main ditch to the depth of two feet, and the depth of eighteen inches in the three-and-a-half feet side drains. If the stones are flat, they can be carefully laid on each other in the bottom of the ditches in such a manner that the water will flow readily through In each case the tops of the stones must be thoroughly covered with shavings, straw, or sod with the grass side down, to prevent the soil from washing in and filling up the space through which the water is to flow.

Tile undoubtedly make the best drains, and are probably cheapest in the long run, even where stone can be had. But we naturally shrink from first cost; and where stone is plenty, its use has the additional advantage of clearing the soil. In many places, however, tile must be employed, and it does the business thoroughly. Mr. Henderson prefers the ordinary horse-shoe tile, and he is a safe man to follow. A good descent must always be provided for, so that the water can flow off rapidly, and the joints of the tile must be covered with sods, the grass side down, or with some other material that will prevent the soil from washing through the slight openings.

Cheap drains can also be made by treading in brush to the depth of two feet and covering as before described. These will remain effective for ten or twelve years, and can be constructed on leased land where the lessee is unwilling to go to great expense. It would be better though to make some arrangement with the landlord, by which both could share the cost of thorough and lasting work.

But let no one say, because my land is leased, or because I only bought to sell again in a few years, it will not pay me to incur the expense of drainage. My best argument on this point will be to relate an incident told by Mr. Henderson in his most excellent work, "Gardening for Profit." He says:

"Every operator in the soil concedes the importance of drainage, yet it is really astonishing to observe how men will work wet lands year after year, wasting annually, by loss of crops, twice the amount required to thoroughly drain. A most industrious German in this vicinity cultivated about eight acres for three years, barely making a living; his soil was an excellent loam, but two-thirds of it was so 'spongy' that he could never get it ploughed till all the neighbors had their crops planted. Driving past one day I hailed him, asking him why he was so late in getting in his crop, when he explained that if he had begun sooner his horses would have 'bogged' so, he might never have got them out again. I suggested draining, but he replied, that would not pay on a leased place; he had started on a leased place which had only seven years more to run, and that he would only be improving it for his landlord, who would allow him nothing for such improvement. After some further conversation, I asked him to jump into my wagon, and in ten minutes we alighted at a market-garden that had six years before been just such a swamp hole as his own, but now (the middle of May) was luxuriant with vegetation. I explained to him what its former condition had been, and that the investing of five hundred dollars in drain tiles would, in twelve months, put his in the same condition. He, being a shrewd man, acted on the advice, and at the termination of his lease, purchased and paid for his eight acres twelve thousand dollars, the savings of six years on his drained garden. I honestly believe, that, had he gone on without draining, he would not have made twelve thousand dollars in twelve years, far less twelve thousand dollars in six years. My friend attributes his whole success in life to our accidental meeting and conversation that May morning, and consequently I have no stancher friend on earth than he."

Thus it will be seen that soils naturally the most favorable for gardening purposes, are often so wet as to make draining indispensable. Where this is the case let the cultivator realize it at once, and waste no time in fighting against Nature. When a loamy piece of land or a muck swamp can be drained, they make the finest garden land existing, and the happy, enterprising owner can be congratulated upon almost certain success; for thorough drainage on one hand avoids the danger of excessive moisture, and the nature of his soil, on the other, enables him to defy drouth.

But if the reader possesses or purchases a loamy soil, that is, a natural mixture of sand and clay, in such proportions that it turns up mellow and friable instead of being sticky and full of stumps, and this is underlaid by a yellow loam subsoil which permits a natural drainage, he may rest satisfied, and commence operations with the first conditions of success in his favor. For here is land of such consistency and compactness that it can be thoroughly and permanently enriched. It is what is termed a "grateful soil." You can bring it up to any degree of fertility, for such portion of the manure dug or ploughed in this year, that is not exhausted by the growth of crops, remains in the soil for use the following season.

Such land is like a good investment that yields its interest every year, and at the same time is growing more valuable. Only by over-cropping and weed-growing, and by under-feeding can such land be impoverished. Yet you will often find ground of this character utterly run out, poor as the spendthrift sandy soils first described, and this because there are so many people, who, in accordance with the old adage, will "ride a willing horse to death." But even when so reduced, I would take such a soil in preference to any other, in view of its grateful character, its saving qualities, so to speak, and its readiness to make liberal return for liberal treatment.

I have also observed that a soil resting on a substratum of slate was peculiarly well adapted to the growth of fruit.

Ordinary clay soils, with good drainage, can be wonderfully and rapidly improved by the use of light stimulating manure, such as the horse stable furnishes, and so treated, are second to none in their yield.

X.

WHEN TO COMMENCE A GARDEN.

"Why, in the spring, of course."

I beg to differ with you, my reader, fair or otherwise. The autumn is the true practical spring in which the gardener should commence operations with the best hopes of success. This may seem paradoxical and contrary to Nature, and save to the comparatively few who have learned by experience, it is at variance with practice. But it is not contrary to Nature, for in the cool dewy nights, and the rains of late August and early September, we have again weather suitable for the stirring of the ground and the sowing and growth of seeds.

WHEN TO COMMENCE A GARDEN.

Much of the garden can again be profitably planted, as we hope to show.

When autumn winds first commence sighing regretfully over the summer season fast departing, and the coming of sere winter, there is a great falling off of interest in the garden on the part of the majority. The spring, with its excitement of hope and promise, the summer, with its satiety of full return, or its disappointment at failure, are nearly past, and the mind is turning to other pursuits and novelties. The garden is neglected, and mainly because it seems to require little attention, and to promise little more for the year. The hardy fruits and vegetables have got so far along that they will mature any way, and not a few who were enthusiastic in April, are now, as far as the garden is concerned, like much in it, on the decline. The number of amateurs who are like what the Bible calls stony-ground hearers, is marvellously large. During hot July their interest dries up, exhales, and their gardens go to the bad.

There is also this somewhat mean tendency in human nature, that when we have got about all out of a person or thing that can be hoped for at present, or when persons are so committed, like a crop nearly matured, that they will give what is expected any way, we are apt to flag in our attentions. Here is where the short-sighted fail, for neither persons nor gardens will continue to commit themselves in our favor under such treatment. I have lost bushels of berries, not in June, the strawberry month, but in August and September, when the beds should have been made and cared for. I have lost hundreds of dollars, not in April and May, but in the autumn, when the seeds of spring crops should have been sown, and in the winter, when they should have been properly protected.

So, then, instead of waiting for spring to commence the campaign of the year, autumn is the time of all others for the provident gardener to enter upon the activities that secure success. Therefore, the value of gardening as a source of recreation or profit, for only about three months of the year are you compelled to comparative idleness.

Because in the strawberry-beds there is nothing but leaves, and among the raspberries only thorns seem to be left, do not neglect them. If you are to have a crop another year, now is the time for action. It is true the melons are on the wane, the cucumbers yellow and dying, the peas like their brush, and the succulent bush-beans going to seed; but is that a reason for giving over these spaces to the dominion of weeds, and leaving them unsightly blemishes upon the garden? God had a right to curse the ground, but I doubt whether we have. And yet I can assure the reader that one thriftless gardener or amateur, whose enthusiasm July has withered, can do more cursing or weed-seeding than half a generation can eradicate. My conscience troubles me not a little in this respect. Apart from the profit there should be principle in the case. Having put our hands to the plough in April, we should not look back in August, because many of our crops are gathered and the thing is becoming an old story.

But having more faith in the profit argument than any based on principle, we hasten to assure the reader again, that if he hopes for continued crops and considerable cash, he must make the most of autumn.

Not to be invidious, or intimate that any of my readers are guilty of such shortcomings, we will suppose a place bought of one of the unregenerate, and the new and agriculturally enlightened owner to be taking possession

Let us go with him, take notes, and watch proceedings. He has wisely bought his place in midsummer, for then in the matured growth of everything he can judge better of the strength and nature of the soil. If there is fruit on the place, he can best learn its character, value, and needs.

As we pass with him from the desert highroad into his promised land, fruitful in great hopes and expectation if nothing else, we observe that many fruit-trees need pruning, and others heading back on account of too rapid growth. Some have been planted closely and are crowding each other; others are suffering from the shade of apparently worthless trees that have grown up around them. On grafted fruit, sprouts and boughs have started below the graft, and are taking all the strength of the root, leaving the good variety to dwindle. For it must be remembered that natural and comparatively worthless fruit grown from the seed, is like the natural man. The wild nature is very apt to get the best of the most approved foreign importation. Thus in the matter of fruit-trees alone there is much to be done before winter, and there is no time for such labors in the rush of spring work

As we pass on, we observe that weeds and bushes, not content with long possession of the fences, are ever encroaching on the open ground. Around the house the hardy perennials and annual bulbs are nearly all past their prime, and withering stalks and sprawling bushes take the place of their early bloom. It is indeed now too late to do much toward enlivening this melancholy domain of flowers with bright and varied annuals or perpetual blooming bedding plants, but it is just the time to see their need, and to commence preparing for its supply another year. At once there

WHEN TO COMMENCE A GARDEN.

is much need for pruning-knife, stake, and twine, that neatness at least may gratify the eye.

But we pass on to the garden. There is scope for any amount of energy in remedying the past and providing for the future.

The raspberries and blackberries are done bearing, but the producing vines are left, drawing their useless life from the strength of the plants, and taking from the growth of the new wood that must produce the following year. Leaving these old vines after they have done bearing, is like tying a horse after a journey, on the side of a hill, where he must stand pulling to no purpose. They will be cut out at once, and not burned, but carried to the compost heap, where, covered with weeds and rubbish they will decay, so that they can be used the following season. Rotted, they will be worth more than their ashes, and the successful gardener is ever looking keenly after fertilizers. The sprawling Black-cap varieties are tied up so that the wood may ripen before winter, and if new plants are wanted, the tips of the vines are slightly covered.

The strawberry-bed is weedy and matted; indeed, all run together. Yet it is worth saving. It is but two years old, and another crop may be had from it. So spaces eighteen inches wide are cut through it, and weeds and plants turned deeply under. By this process, rows a foot in width are left between the spaces, and these must be weeded by hand. Or, if the bed is sufficiently extended, the same process can be performed by a plough, a space of three feet being turned under, and another of plants eighteen inches wide left for fruiting. If the bed has become very full of grass or white clover, it will be turned under at once, and a new one set out elsewhere.

There is a space that was planted in early peas. The vines are still sprawling about or clinging to the old bush. Unless the latter are of cedar, or of some good hard wood, the whole rubbish is swept away to the compost heap. The ground is then clear and can be prepared for a fall or spring crop. If July has not passed, and good strong celery plants can be had, these may be set out at once. If it is about the 10th of August, the early yellow-stone or strap-leaved turnips can still be sown. But we will even suppose August on the wane, and that our new and eager purchaser can do little more with his ground that can make any return this year.

Still, having read some better book than this, or having had his eyes opened by experience, his own or that of some one else, he does not dream of waiting till the following spring, but with hearty vigor, commences at once.

Those old withering cucumber-vines are swept

away, and the flourishing weeds with them. If the ground is rich, sloping, with excellent drainage, he can sow onion seed there immediately, and market the crop in April following. The early potatoes are dug, or can be, and thus there is a place to set out a new strawberry-bed. The sweet corn will be out of the way this month. He will not leave the earless stalks to wither, and dry up where they stand. Here and there one may be left with an exceedingly fine ear for seed. But with the rest, as fast as the ears are used, the stalks will go to the cows, or if he has none, they will be buried in their green succulent state, under the compost heap. Well buried too; or else, even though half the garden were planted in mignonette, the decaying corn, so sweet and wholesome in life, will now render the region anything but savory. The land thus cleared will no doubt be sown with spinach. Then there is ground where early cabbage and cauliflower were grown. The onions are dry enough to gather, the bush-beans are past their prime, and if not desired for use in their dry state, they also can be swept away. The late and refuse pods that are left after the vines have been picked over many times do not contain seed fit for planting.

Thus here and there through the garden spaces can be cleared which may be sown with spinach, dwarf German greens, or " sprouts," or set out with small refuse onions that will be fit for market in their green state, in April and May following. In early September lettuce can be sown and wintered over as will hereafter be explained. This last-named vegetable, properly managed, can be made very profitable, if partially grown in the fall. The same is true of cabbage and cauliflower plants kept over through the winter for early planting. No amount of effort and expense with hot-beds in February and March can secure plants that will mature as early for market as those preserved from the preceding season in cold frames.

Thus we have seen the new and enlightened possessor of a neglected place go to work in the autumn as zealously as do the majority in spring, and when spring comes he is two or three months in advance of his neighbors. While they are breaking up and planting their ground at great expense, and are compelled to wait till midsummer for returns, he is selling crops wintered over, thus meeting the heavy drafts upon his purse entailed by the extra work and outlay of the opening season.

When the dying leaves begin to fall in October, my garden is almost as green with growing crops as in the following May, and usually I have been able to winter them over without great difficulty. Thus, instead of waiting till June and July before receiving anything from my ground, my sales on the last day of April amounted to one hundred and seventeen dollars, and on the last of May to two hundred and eighty dollars. The heavy and unusual expenses of spring were therefore partially met in the spring.

It is true that farther to the north and on cold, wet soils the difficulty of wintering over crops would be much greater; but it is also true that in light soils and sheltered locations farther south, the facility of so doing would be much greater than in our latitude. So much in favor of an autumn rather than a spring commencement of a garden already in a fair state of cultivation.

But if the reader has taken a new piece of ground that must be broken in for the first time, the argument for this course is doubly strong. If he waits till spring he almost loses a year. If there are stones, rocks, bushes, or stumps upon it, he cannot clear it up in spring sufficiently early to raise much that season, but in the long autumn months he can work marvellous changes Even if we have nothing more to contend with than a stiff sod on the land, great advantages are secured by breaking it up in autumn. If this is done in August, it will rot sufficiently by November to permit deep cross ploughing. The decay of the sod can be greatly hastened by giving it a coating of stable manure before it is turned under, and at the same time it will go far toward giving the land the necessary degree of fertility. For it must be remembered that no field, however good its condition for farm crops, is rich enough for the exactions of garden, nor can one year's culture, nor the highest degree of fertilizing bring it into a proper state. Under the best management it requires time. But we gain almost a year if we commence in autumn. In the first place the heavy coat of manure upon the sod assists greatly in its decay. By the edge of winter both are ready to crumble into soil and the ground can be thoroughly and deeply cross-ploughed. This gives the frost a chance to sweeten and pulverize it. In the spring it should be again well enriched, ploughed deeply, and planted in early potatoes, sweet corn, peas, and similar summer crops that would secure good cultivation. By July and August these crops are gathered and your land is clear. Again manure it heavily, plough deeply, very deeply with a "lifting subsoil plough," and now your ground can be laid out as you desire, and in one short year will be in as high a state of culture and fertility as the majority of gardens around you.

Still if you are bent on grand success, you will not be half satisfied, but by most liberal cultivation will secure increasingly large returns as the years roll on.

By the course described, however, you can lay out your garden in accordance with your approved plan in the autumn following your commencement, and the summer crops as described will go far toward paying the expenses of the first year. In August and September your strawberry-beds can be set, spring crops planted, and in October, cold frames made, raspberries, blackberries, currants, trees, and grape-vines set out, and you are fairly launched.

XI.

WE WILL GO TO WORK.

Perhaps we have talked long enough on general principles, suggestions at large, and had now better go practically to work and produce that two thousand dollars announced in the opening chapter. I will commence consistently with my theory, in August of '70, but will speak only of such operations as brought returns the following year.

Our old-fashioned one o'clock dinner is over, and books now mean dyspepsia, but gardening, as I practise it, is health. In the first place, I repair to the ancient central apple-tree to provide strategy.

Manufacturing it, as did the generals of the

old school, I sit down before the problem. It is not necessary that my forces should assume this contemplative attitude also. They can work away at those Philistines, the weeds, wherever they show themselves, while I develop such definite, decisive steps as are possible to one also burdened with the duty of digesting a dinner. The mid-day sun is still intense, and I progress with my strategy with an eye to its westward decline. But as the vertical rays cease, as the cool shadows creep eastward, I step forth from my retirement with the air of one resolved. I determine, in the first place, upon making a strawberry-bed that will astonish the natives. Here is a suitable piece of ground from which some early crop has been taken. It is in the main a sandy loam, a little too light in some places but fair throughout. Having had it thoroughly cleared, leaving not a sprig of white clover or sorrel, for however deep you bury them they are apt to work out and grow (perhaps they always do, on the China side, if not this), I then directed Thomas to cover it with four inches of the very best manure. This was an exceedingly heavy coat, far more than is usually necessary, but I was bent on producing some extraordinary results. My genial landlord, Mr. David, and another neighbor happening to pass, indulged in some pleasantries as to the flavor of strawberries raised under the circumstances, but I knew well that Nature, with ten months to work in, was too skilful an alchemist to make any such mistakes. So the limited piece of ground was dug very deeply and made almost as rich as a hot-bed. Then commenced the gradual setting of plants, gradual, because it was a dry time, and the sun still scorchingly hot at mid-day. Therefore I directed that the plants should be set out only in the evening, a few at a time, and well watered. Afterwards they were shaded during the heat of the day till they became well rooted and could take care of themselves. This shade can be provided by leaning a board over a row supporting it by a couple of stakes or small stones. If appearances are not regarded, old raspberry bushes, pea-vines, anything that will shade the young plants without smothering them, will answer. The relief given by a little shade is wonderful, and plants will grow in the hottest weather when so protected. Where the variety is valuable and scarce, they should always be so treated when set out in a warm, dry time.

Of course, if I could have made my bed just before a good shower or a night's rain, no such precautions would have been needed, and the plants would have grown without further care.

"Why not wait then till the shower comes?" some may ask.

When will it come? Yet many days perhaps.

Or it may be when I am away, and I, instead of my plants, will be caught in it. Or it will beat its musical tattoo on the roof after you are gone to bed. What can you then do about it? More than likely it will come on Sunday, and even in this lax age of Sabbath keeping, setting out a strawberry-bed would hardly be esteemed an act of " necessity or mercy." " He that regardeth the clouds shall not reap," nor get his strawberry-bed made in due season. The earlier you can set your plants in summer or fall the better your crop the following season, and I determined to lose not a day in starting mine and assisting Nature through the " dry-spell." At the same time, if the rain comes, the provident gardener will do his best to make the most of it. If he intends setting out plants he will have them ready, and the ground also, and then when the western horizon darkens, and the mutter of distant thunder is heard, or when the east wind comes sighing in from the ocean, the avant courier of the coming storm, he makes every moment tell in the putting out of plants, knowing that the refreshing rain-drops can do more for them in one hour than can be done by days of shading and watering. But with us the thunder gusts seem to hide behind the mountains till all prepared, and then to swoop down so suddenly that we are flying for shelter from the big drops before we realized that they were coming. Only too often they raise their black heads in the west, and seem coming right down upon us with such abundant promise that hope and expectation are raised to the highest pitch; then suddenly, as if attracted by some blue Highland in the distance, they appear to change their minds, and, like the Levite in the parable, "pass by on the other s'de." If, beguiled by hopes of a shower, you have set out plants largely, then watering and shading is your only chance of saving them. My plan, as I have said, was to set out a few plants every night and take care of them, to have plants and ground ready, and then if there came rain to get out beforehand as many as possible. When my bed was half filled it did come, and by prompt action the rest of the ground was covered in time to catch the precious drops. But those first set out were growing vigorously in spite of dry weather, and after the rain they went forward with a bound, far exceeding the others.

By the first of September, therefore, my bed was filled with strong and thrifty plants of the following varieties: Two rows of the Wilson, two of Durand Seedling, one of the Russell, one of the Agriculturist, two of the Triomphe de Gand, and one of the Jucunda. I thought by placing the celebrated varieties side by side under specially favorable culture, I might learn which was the best. The result with all was astonishing. A soldier who saw a basket of them thought they were tomatoes. The Wilsons of course bore the largest number, and the berries also were very large, but many of the other named varieties were simply monstrous, and they all seemed nearly equal in this instance in vigor and productiveness, except the Jucundas, and though these bore as large berries as any, the vines were rather feeble and inclined to die out. For large, showy berries, few, if any, surpass the Jucundas, and with high culture on a heavy soil, and kept rigorously in hills, they will produce fruit that will stop a man running for a train, should it meet his eye. At a fashionable Broadway fruit store, they would bring almost any price asked, but they would be like many of their wealthy purchasers, rather insipid and hollow. As grown in my grounds their flavor is not to be mentioned in the same week with the Russell and Triomphe. Still they are growing in favor, especially as a market-berry, and doubtless are just the thing grown in hills on heavy land.

The Durand Seedling has not done as well with me as it at first promised. Its foliage has seemed somewhat delicate and unable to endure the hot sun, and though producing some very large fruit, many of the blossoms failed, and in shade the berries would "damp off" and decay. But with careful hill culture on light soils, I should think it might prove one of the best among the large varieties. The fruit of the Agriculturist also tended somewhat to scalding and decay, but with open row or hill culture on a light soil it does wonders. As grown upon the bed described, the Russell would make one of the finest varieties in existence, if it were only a little firmer. Summing up the results of the experiment, it may be said that the Wilsons gave the largest yield, while in view of their firmness, size, as well as the other good qualities, the Triomphes perhaps bore away the palm.

But I can emphatically assure the reader that the first crop upon the bed, though made with so much pains and cost, more than paid all expenses. At the close of this chapter I will also describe another crop raised upon the same ground at the same time.

I give the issue of this little experiment in this place in order that it may stand in direct connection with the rather elaborate preparation, and satisfy the reader that unusual outlay will often secure unusual return. But my special reason for so doing is to show that strawberry-beds set out in autumn will give a handsome crop the following season, thus saving a year to the impatient gardener, and the gain of a year even in the matter of strawberries is no trifling matter in our transient life. I admit that on most soils, and under most circumstances, the plants are more certain to grow if set out in early spring. If I had to buy my vines at a distance, or was about to invest in some new and costly variety, I should prefer spring by all means. But if I had plenty of young plants in my own garden, or could obtain them of a near neighbor, I should be equally in favor of summer and fall planting. Vines set out in spring will produce nothing worth speaking of that season, and should not be permitted to bear at all, whereas by early summer planting, and the extra care possible in a small garden, a large crop can be had the following June. For instance, my strong plants commence throwing out runners rapidly even in June while fruiting. If I were anxious to obtain new runners, and made the ground rich and mellow around the producing plants, there would be plenty fit for transplanting in early July. As we have before described, there are many spaces throughout the garden that were occupied by early potatoes, peas, etc., which can now be cleared up and set out with strawberries. Two of my finest beds for '73 were set out last July. Thus, from a small bed of good strong plants, runners can be taken for transplanting from 4th of July till the middle of October, and as fast as crops mature in summer they can be gathered, and the land, if desired, can at once be occupied with this most delicious small fruit. I had in '72 a small bed, fifteen feet by thirty, of a very choice kind, one indeed that promises better than any I ever raised (I have tried at least twenty varieties), and from this limited area I obtained plants enough, without special effort, to set out a large portion of my garden before October, besides many which were given away. I made my rows two feet apart, and early plantings were set out two and three feet from each other in the row; but those vines put out in July and August also threw out runners, and by October filled the rows close up with plants. If I had not been anxious to produce new vines, I would not have permitted this, as the young beds would have been much stronger, and in better condition for bearing, if all runners had been cut from them. It is true that this variety is the most vigorous grown on my soil that I have ever seen. Having once marked its dark-green foliage, its red stocky leaf-stems and runners, you would always recognize it afterwards even at a distance. Much of its fruit was immensely large, and even the last pickings from my small bed were of good size. I do not know its name with certainty, but think it is a new berry, known as Boydan's No. 30. In the spring of '70 I obtained a few plants of six new varieties, and put them out in row. side by side. A man weeding them carelessly carried off the labels, so I was able to distinguish only one kind, the Kentucky Seedling. In '71 they all fruited finely, but none proved so satisfactory as this unknown friend who had lost his name. But true worth will assert itself under all circumstances, while the utmost flourish in title will not long shield the unworthy or common-place. I promoted the stranger by digging up all the others save the Kentucky, and giving him a chance to "spread himself," which he immediately did, proving that, like the successful men of the world, he only wanted half a chance. In the summer of '71, I set out a small bed of this variety, and in '72 obtained a wonderful yield from the same. The berry is grown on tall fruit stalks, but which are unable to sustain the weight of the enormous berries. Therefore they should be mulched, that is, straw, leaves, or green grass cut in summer, should be placed around the plants. This keeps the ground around them moist, greatly enhances the crop, and also prevents the fruit from lying on the ground, thus becoming covered with earth and grit. The berries have a long neck, making the hulling process easy; they are firm, solid, with a rich crimson flush throughout.

As I have said, I was so pleased with this variety, that in the summer and fall of '72 I set out a large portion of my garden with it, and should it turn out as well another season, one need not ask a more profitable business than raising them. Mr. Thomas Skene is trying this variety in the greenhouse this winter, and so by spring we will know its value for forcing.

As before intimated, another crop equally fragrant, and perhaps taking the world at large almost an equal favorite, was raised at the same time on the strawberry-bed described above. I refer to the aromatic onion. As soon as the rows were filled with plants in '70, the little black seed of the large red, and the yellow

Danvers varieties were sown between them. At that warm season it was but a few days before the little onions were pricking through the soil thick as hair. I had ordered plenty of seed sown, knowing that the plants would have to run the gauntlet of the winter frosts. Indeed, the whole thing was an experiment, for I never knew of its being done in our latitude, and could find no instruction in the books on the subject. Nevertheless, the presumptuous onions grew sturdily on, without the countenance of any "authority" or known precedent, and in winter they varied in height from six inches to one foot. The same covering put over the strawberry-bed also protected them, and in spring they nearly all came out as bright as if they had only had a good nap, and were just wakened. Then a spirit of emulation seemed to spring up between them and the strawberry vines. Side by side, "neck and neck," they went forward together. Many laughed to see these rather dissimilar products of nature growing so amicably in company. But the strawberry, with an inherent, not a borrowed nobility, "put on no airs" towards its useful and humble neighbor. The same warm winter covering sheltered both. They both drew from one enriched soil the elements of prosperity. In brief, the conditions that were favorable for one were also for both, and side by side they went on and developed in accordance with their own laws and nature, thus setting an excellent example to the wealthy and working classes. Indeed, that intermingled strawberry and onion bed was a profound essay on political economy, teaching that all classes can prosper together, not by becoming alike, and reducing society to dreary monotony, but by each one carrying out without hindrance or prejudice its own germinal character in the most pronounced diversity.

That is a wretched soil that only suits one genus of plants. In an equally miserable condition is that society where only one class prospers, even though in its conceit it calls itself the " best class."

In imagination I see some pseudo-political economist, some champion of the development of the upper-class, at the expense of all the others, bristling with indignation, and perhaps purple with offended pride.

"I don't believe in such associations," he exclaims haughtily. "Your plebeian onions will affect the flavor of the patrician strawberry, just as the upper classes tone down and deteriorate as they mingle with inferiors. Separation, sir, separation—Chinese walls—these are the hope of blue blood."

"Your premise is false, sir, as it usually is, and therefore your conclusion is wrong. The onion growing by the strawberry has no influence on its flavor whatever. Your artificial noblemen no doubt need careful nursing and 'Chinese walls;' but those who have received their patent from Heaven will develop as noblemen and live as such under all circumstances, even as my Triomphes produced the most luscious vinous-flavored fruit, though a thrifty onion grew a few inches away."

But I am wandering. The garden is so suggestive of all kinds of truth that one can hardly help it. I suppose that is the reason the first man was placed in one, since in learning gardening he would learn almost everything else.

I will immediately descend from political economy and social science to onions, a long descent some may think, and yet in *strength* this theme will out*rank* most others.

I will close with a few practical sentences befitting this useful but much abused vegetable

It was my expectation that the onions between the strawberry rows would be out of the way long before the fruit was ripe, and so they were, save a few I left purposely to see what they would come to. Even in March my gardener commenced pulling and selling them in their green state, and by May 1st nearly all were gone, realizing the snug sum of forty dollars. This is a phase of the subject at which even the most aristocratic will not elevate their noses. The space occupied by them was exceedingly small. It was their earliness, their large green succulent tops, and tendency to make good-sized bulbs, that secured such prompt sale at high prices. They stood very thickly in the rows, and as the largest were daily culled out, those remaining grew rapidly, and filled their places.

Those that I left to mature went to seed, just as a large bulb set out in the spring will, and when dry the strength of the bulbs had gone into the seed, and the former were large but useless. If, however, the seed-stalk had been cut away and the bulbs used in their green state, they would have been most excellent. I was thus satisfied that a *very* early and profitable crop of onions could be raised from seed sown in August.

My next experiment was to sow the seed late in September, so that the plants would not be large enough in spring to run up to seed, but develop large bulbs, as in the case with seed sown in April. If the plants would winter over, no matter how small they were, the crop would be far earlier than any that could be started with the opening season, unless it be from what are termed "sets" or little onions put out as soon as the frost is gone. But I found it would not answer. Unless the seed was sown in August, the plants did not gain size, vigor, and root-power enough to resist the winter. Farther to the south though, on warm light soils, I should think this might be done to great advantage. But after so much onion the reader is probably ready to take a tearful farewell of this chapter.

XII.

THE CAMPAIGN IN SEPTEMBER.

THERE are few months in the year more attractive than September. It reminds you of that alliterative description of the matured lady, "fair, fat, and forty;" and he is but a shallow-brained man who has not found this class one of the most attractive in society. There is a beauty of autumn as well as of spring, of age, as of youth. I have great hopes of that boy who is enamored by a lady "old enough to be his mother." He has an aspiring soul that dimly recognizes something far beyond itself and will never sink satisfied into mediocrity. When such a woman grows old gracefully, sweetened and ripened in character by the action of time, she is a most charming companion for all. The infirmities of age have not come, but she knows that they are near, and her sympathies instinctively go out to those who are (as she soon will be) bending under the burden of years Her memory of youth is still strong, and she turns to it, and to those in its enjoyment, with a remorseful tenderness, as the emigrant looks back to a loved familiar, but fading shore. The fitful waywardness, the April skies of youth, the intense feelings and passions of midsummer life, are passing into the calm and content of early autumn. She is, like the season, in a border land between two dissimilar states, and having some of the characteristics of both.

Flecks of gray in the "bonny brown hair" may awaken regretful thoughts of the approaching frostiness of age, just as in early September there comes sighing through the trees a wind that speaks so plainly of the fading year, that we are saddened in spite of ourselves. But when through all experiences she has kept a young heart, it will often show itself in a sprightliness, a spring-like, youthful manner, just as many days in September remind you of May. Thus the lady past her prime, that in the ordinary stock novel is so generally sneered at, may be a most gracious, lovely personage. The memory of her trials and temptations in youth, the struggles and burdens of middle age on one hand, give her the broadest, deepest charity for those still passing through these ordeals; while on the other, with strength undiminished, as yet, she can stay the tottering steps of age with a peculiar and sympathetic tenderness. The graces of her mind and character are like the flowers of autumn. There is no longer the growth of immature foliage and wood, but all the strength of the plant goes into rich and varied bloom. The garden is spring-like again with all its abundant blossoms, but the flowers are larger, deeper, and richer in their coloring, more perfect in their form than ever before. The drooping annuals make a sudden rapid growth, all the "bedding-plants" cover themselves with renewed beauty. Pansies, that in hot August were wee "johnny-jumpers," become pansies again, with great staring, human-like faces. The turf grows greener and more velvety, and all nature seems to say, Let us have one more blessed thrill of life before the frosts of death fall. Make the most of September, for you will have nothing like it till May comes round again. Alas! May comes but once in human life, and even to the bravest and most beautiful, autumn must grow sere and sad painfully fast, when there is no hope of the "glory that fadeth not away." Such may well cling to September.

"Bother all this!" growls some practical reader, "I want you to tell me how to plant spinach."

And so my sentiment becomes sandwiched between an onion and spinach-bed. The interruption has thoroughly clipped my wings, and the rest of the chapter shall be satisfactory even to old Money Bags himself.

Spinach should be sown from the 1st to the 15th of this month, and in our latitude I should have the best expectations from seed put in the ground during the first week. Plants that have had time to attain good size, with strong long roots, winter over the best; and where you can commence selling a good crop in April it is very profitable. No great skill is required to raise spinach. Richness of soil is the main necessity for either a summer or winter crop. Like all vegetables grown for their foliage, it must make a rapid growth to be good. Therefore it succeeds best on a deep, moist soil, but one thoroughly drained, where no water or ice stands during the winter. I sow my seed about an inch deep, and find great advantage in covering it with a half-inch or more of well-rotted manure. This gives it a fine start, and seems to prevent in some degree the unfavorable action of frost. I have used the Round-leaved variety, and believe it is regarded as the best both for fall and spring sowing. If there is any moisture in the ground, the seed comes up quickly, and, as with all vegetables, the use of the hoe hastens the growth.

I plant my rows a foot apart and the seed quite thickly in the row. Then in spring you cut for use in such a way as to thin out, and the remaining plants by their rapid growth will fill up the space as fast as it is made, so that the bed seems like the "widow's cruse of oil," constantly drawn upon, but not diminishing.

But I seldom make a spinach-bed by itself, using instead the intervening spaces between other things. I put a row or two between my hardy raspberries, blackcaps, and blackberries. Where I make a new strawberry-bed in summer, I sow spinach in September between the rows. The same covering and manure answers for both, and as the rows are two feet apart, and the spinach is marketed in April, they do not interfere with each other. This should only be done the first fall, and on highly enriched land: after that the strawberries should have all to themselves. But in the fall and spring of '70–71, I raised fine crops in this way, and by the time winter commenced in '72 there must have been ten or fifteen barrels of spinach growing on my new strawberry-beds. The heavy body of snow has protected it so far, and if the spring is favorable, it will all be marketed by the end of the first week in May.

In addition to what was used in the family in the spring of '71, there were thirty-one and one-fourth bushels sold, realizing forty-six dollars and sixty-four cents. In the following fall, little seed was sown, and that was nearly all killed out by the hard open winter. But the fall of '72 promised a crop double in amount to any I have raised before.

The seed of another vegetable belonging to the Kale family is also sown in September, and its culture and treatment is the same as that of spinach. Dwarf German greens or "sprouts" is the variety that succeeds best, and has the readiest sale. Its foliage resembles that of the Ruta-baga Turnip, and it is cut and used in the spring precisely as spinach. Its flavor is like that of the cabbage, but more delicate, and coming when vegetables are scarce, it adds to the variety, and is welcome. Wherever there are Germans there is no difficulty in selling it, and Mr. Henderson states that sometimes in the vicinity of New York it yields a crop worth five hundred dollars per acre. Sometimes I succeed in wintering it over very nicely; then again it dies out. It requires a light soil and a covering of very coarse litter during the coldest weather. In the spring of '71, nine and a half bushels were sold for twelve dollars—I mention the sales of spinach and kale, in connection with their description and mode of cultivation, as space will permit me to refer to them but briefly hereafter. It will be seen that the prices were high, compared with New York market, but my gardener sold the bulk at retail, or in small quantities, and so received the sum named.

I think most gardeners would find it very profitable to raise these vegetables, especially spinach. If their ground were light, sloping, and very rich, their success would be almost certain and at little cost. And yet, even farmers do not raise these crops to any extent, and in April, when vegetables are so few, a prompt remunerative sale might be counted upon in any locality.

The next vegetable started in the fall to which I shall refer, is Lettuce, and with me it has been one of the most important of the entire season. I have sown the seed with the best success from the 10th to the 20th of September. Any fair garden ground will answer, as it must be taken up and protected in cold frames the latter part of October. This process will be described in the next chapter. Therefore the fall operation consists only in raising the small plants, and this does not require much ground. The rows can be sown eight inches apart, and the only cultivation needed is to keep the ground loose and free from weeds. But the selection of the right varieties is very important; and as Burr describes fifty-three kinds, including the Cos species, and as the seed catalogues are not so far behind him in their bewildering profusion of candidates for favor, it will be seen that the choice is not "Hobson's." And yet success depends upon selecting rightly. Mr. Henderson tells us how he lost his entire crop of early lettuce (a very important one) by sowing, through mistake, the best summer, instead of the best spring variety.

As the favorite kind for wintering over in cold frames, the Early Curled Simpson may be named. It does not make a head, but forms a large, close, compact mass of leaves, and is delightfully crisp and delicate in flavor after its rapid spring growth. It is very hardy, and I have succeeded well in wintering it over in the open ground with a slight covering. This should be the main crop for fall sowing. I have also used three other varieties to great advantage. First, the Green Winter, which is very hardy, and will generally stand the severest cold. It makes a fine head early in spring, but soon runs up to seed. The Tennis Ball is a small but most excellent variety, and makes a very compact head. For home use it is unsurpassed, and it is one of the best for forcing in cold frames, as it takes up so little room. The heads can be grown six inches apart each way. For a second crop in the spring I find great advantage in wintering over a large number of the Black Seeded Butter variety. Strong plants grown the previous fall attain large size in May in the open ground. Nothing started in hot-beds in February or March can compete with them. By the first week of June, this kind makes a head almost as large as a cabbage, white and very tender and delicate.

It is always well to try to winter some plants over out of doors. If they die, the loss is slight, as the seed and labor cost nothing worth mentioning. Select a warm sheltered place in the garden where no ice or water will stand, and sow about September 10th some seed of each of the four varieties named, especially of the Green Winter. When the ground begins to freeze hard, cover with cedar boughs or some very coarse litter. Anything that will settle down closely on the plants will cause them to decay. They may come out in the spring almost equal to those in the cold frames. As soon as the frost is out, they can be taken up and forced under glass, or set in the open ground, where, from their hardiness, they will soon mature for market.

In the same manner as lettuce the seed of cabbage or cauliflower can be sown in the fall. In our latitude it should not be planted earlier than the 5th of September, or the plants will run up to seed in the spring instead of making heads; nor later than the 20th, for then they will be too small to stand the winter. Like lettuce, they can be started in a small bed anywhere in the garden, and left to grow to the middle or latter part of October, when they must be removed to cold frames, as will be hereafter described. I would advise that a good sprinkling of lime be raked into the land on which the seed is to be sown, and that the cultivator see to it that none of the Cabbage family, and also that neither turnips nor radishes have grown on the ground of his seed-bed for a year or two previous. Where this has been the case, his plants will be very apt to contract a disease known as club-root, and though lime is a preventative, he would have no certainty against failure. His only safety is to use lime or bone-dust freely, and to sow his seed where nothing has been grown for two or three years that seems to draw the insect so fatal to the Cabbage tribe.

As to the best varieties for wintering over, the Jersey Wakefield is the favorite around New York. I have had very good success with it. The head is of fair size, and the outer leaves are so few that it requires but little room, and can be set two feet apart each way, or even a little closer if ground is scarce. The Early York matures as quickly, but is nothing like as large, and the Wakefield, if abundant, would drive it from the market. When the Early Ox Heart heads well, it is superior in quality to the others. As a succession coming into market two or three weeks later than the kinds named, the early Flat Dutch and the Winningstadt can be recommended. The latter is a very large, solid cabbage, and one that can be depended on in good soil. For a village or local market, we would not advise the gardener to go largely into cauliflower, for the majority in the country will not pay much more for this delicious vegetable than for a coarse head of cabbage, and as a crop it is very uncertain. If one has soil suitable for it, and can develop a demand at high prices, it will pay well. Early Erfurt and Early Parris are perhaps the best for wintering over.

I have also tried the experiment of sowing beet seed in the fall, but without much success. Noticing that some small beets left in the old bed during the winter developed into large roots *very early* in the season, it occurred to me that by sowing the seed in September they might live till the following spring, and would then be fit for market in May, when they would bring a large price. A few survived, but the majority died under the severe frost. I do not think my plants attained sufficient size before winter, and perhaps with greater care in covering more would have lived. At any rate, I was not satisfied with the experiment, and shall **try it** again. Farther south I should think it might be done with great success.

It is natural that I should come round again to the globular onion. Is there not a weakness in fallen humanity for this ancient vegetable? The "Chosen People" loathed the "light bread," the manna from Heaven, but "wept" regretfully at the thought of the "onion." Some fair theologians may regard this as proof that there has been a sad breaking down in human nature. (I wonder if they never eat onions sliced in vinegar on the sly, when no callers are expected. The cynical world is so suspicious of the indignant disgust at onions.) Did they grow in Eden? Could they have been the forbidden fruit? Certainly no modern garden of fallen man is regarded as complete without them. How strong must have been those of Egypt when a whole nation wept at the very thought of them!

Despise not the onion, Miss Angelica. It is classical, nay, more, it is sacred. Behold the most venerable nation of the world in tears—"the people weeping throughout their families, every man in the door of his tent." What was the touching cause. Memory—memory of the past—past "leeks, onions, and garlic."

Through the *leeks*, Hebrew patriotism, fortitude, and faith oozed out, and unmanned, they wept aloud. Thus the associations of mystery, antiquity, and sentiment, as well as deepest emotion, centre in this odorous bulb. Cease, then, Angelica—cease, artificial society, thy unjust and too often assumed contempt for the onion. Let us be true.

Braced by these historical memories, and the record of sales on my cash-book, I shall boldly refer to the onion whenever occasion requires; and I now proceed to state I have found great advantage in putting many of my "sets" (small onions) in the ground during September and at any time when convenient. I use the largest of my sets in this manner—those that would go to seed in the spring any way, and also any refuse onions that I have or can buy at slight cost. Occasionally rows of this vegetable attaining but little size have not been used, and I have simply let them stand during the season. In August their tops die down, but in the moist, cool weather of September they start and grow again, and even go ahead of those set out, and by winter are strong plants. I then have the ground *between* them covered with light and partly decayed manure, and this keeps the frost from heaving them out. The plants themselves should not be covered deeply with anything, or they will decay. A little very coarse litter in the coldest weather is all that is necessary. From beds so treated the onions were fit for market in their green state by the 25th of March in '71.

Let the practical reader smack his lips over the closing flavor of this chapter, and forget the sentiment in the opening pages.

XIII.

PREPARING FOR WINTER QUARTERS.

OCTOBER has come, bringing labors abundant in the garden. Every day now may be made to tell, not only on the success of the coming summers, but of coming years. But work is play in the cool, brilliant days of this most beautiful month, and every inhalation of the bracing air over the fresh-turned earth means health and longer life. If ministers and brain-workers generally could manage to spend October in the varied labors now required in their own gardens, they would not break down much under a century. I say their own, for I doubt whether the exercise would be as beneficial in some one else's garden. The work might be the same, but a certain zest would be wanting, just as a glass of cider is rather flat without its sparkle and carbonic acid gas. Even ministers have not reached that point of disinterestedness which would enable them to work in a neighbor's garden with the same zeal and pleasure, and therefore the same benefit, as in their own. Exercise that is taken mechanically with no heart or enjoyment, does a man no more good than the running of a machine does it. It simply tends to wear out. I have seen good men solemnly sawing wood before breakfast to strengthen their constitution. I fear only iron constitutions can bear such tonics. I once tried it myself in student days, and the result was backache, headache, and general prostration. Exercise in the way of recreation must give employment to the mind as well as the body, and must be of a kind that, as the children say, is "fun" to us. It should be performed *con amore*. Otherwise it becomes but another phase of wearing work. I am satisfied that the Good Father meant that His children should play not a little all through their earthly lives, and if grave men and women played more, they could do more and better work. Why should not men play? Don't old apple-trees blossom as well as the daisies? Wearing toil was never meant for unfallen man, and yet Adam and Eve were gardeners from the first. (For I am satisfied that Eve did not sit in a bower and read novels all day while Adam "delved," and we know she did not spend her time in dressing.) Therefore, on our cursed thistle-growing earth, may we not find in the garden hints of that labor that rests body and soul—labor having more enjoyment than wanton frolic? Come with me into my garden and see, even when preparing for winter, instead of spring with its promise, and summer with its ripe fulfilment.

We will first mow the asparagus bed and burn the dying tops, for if the seeds of this most delicious vegetable (in its place) become scattered, they make a troublesome weed. Now cover the bed with two or three inches of stable manure, and it is done for till the following spring.

No frosts have fallen yet, but they are nightly expected, therefore we must be ready. The beets had better be gathered in at once and placed in a cool cellar, as frost injures them. I have found that by putting my roots in a barrel and covering them with six inches of fresh earth, it prevented them from wilting. It has been my custom to plant bush-beans in early August, in odd places, where early crops have matured. By the last of September and the first week of October, the vines are full of green tender pods. These put away in pickle will keep till beans come again, and when properly freshened and prepared for the table, you can scarcely tell them in February and March from those just picked.

In some places they would also find a ready sale in the fall, though out of season. We find the limas full of green but well-filled pods. One slight frost would spoil them all, but if picked before it, and spread thin on the garret floor, they will make one of our best winter vegetables. We will give the late cabbage and cauliflower one more good hoeing, and pull out any that are diseased. The carrots should be taken up before the ground begins to freeze. and the squashes gathered before the frost touches them. The celery is growing fast now, the cool weather just suiting it, and therefore every few days it should be well earthed up so that the blanching process may go on with the growth. Select a few well-loaded tomato-vines and egg-plants in some sheltered place, if possible, and be prepared to cover them well in case of a cold night. I have known all the vines to be killed by one frost in early October, and then there was no frost till quite late in November. If a few vines could have been protected through that one cold snap, they would have supplied the family with tomatoes a month longer. The late supply can also be eked out by hanging up a few well-filled vines in a dry, sunny place, in some out-building or attic, and they will gradually ripen their fruit. Turnips will make their chief growth in this month, and it is always better to have them in rows, so that they can be often hoed. Keep the spinach, kale, and onions growing rapidly by frequent cultivation.

And now we come to the main and special work of the season, preparation for the future. First we will remember those sweet friends that have brightened our eyes all summer. Flower seeds will be gathered and labelled, plants that we wish to preserve will now be put in pots, tender bulbs, such as the tube rose and gladiolus, taken up and stowed in a cool, dry place. Then, that spring may be doubly welcomed, we will make our crocus, tulip, and hyacinth beds. The two last named should be planted four inches deep, and the smaller bulbs about half the distance. When severe frosts commence, some coarse litter should be thrown over the beds. Space will not permit me to go into the subject of flowers to that degree that inclination prompts. Moreover, the mercenary phase of these papers rather forbids it, as my play has been so closely linked with profit. But I can refer the reader to a charming practical little book, by Miss Warner, and published by Randolph & Co. If one can read that without sending to Mr. Vick, or some one, for flower seeds and bulbs, it may be doubted whether he (or she) is descended from Adam. We will, therefore, return to those products of the garden that appeal to the grosser sense of taste.

Currant and gooseberry bushes should now be pruned; that is, old, half-dead wood cut out, and all trimmed into shape. If more plants are desired, cuttings from the new wood, grown during the past summer, can be made and set out about a foot apart in the row. The cuttings may be from five to eight inches in length, and should be put in the ground about four inches, and the soil made firm around them. They then may be left to grow one or two seasons, according to convenience, and afterwards put where they are to fruit. Good soil, freedom from weeds, and liberal use of pruning knife, are all that the currant and gooseberry ask in order to make regular and full returns. Strong plants may also be had by bending the bushes down and covering them partially with earth, or better still, heaping the soil up around them in the fall, and then every stalk will not only bear fruit, but will throw out roots, and the whole bush may be divided in the following October into a half a dozen or more vigorous new plants.

Now is the time, also, to put out the bushes where they are expected to grow for years to come; and as they can be had at no great cost, it would be well for those who have none to get their first supply at the nursery. It is true, as we have said, that currants will grow in neglected corners, along fences, anywhere that its roots can get half a hold upon the soil, but it is also true that it will make double return in thoroughly enriched garden soil. It is a fruit that a slovenly cultivator can depend upon, but also one that the careful gardener can do wonders with. The currant worm is proving a formidable enemy in some districts, but Mr. Skene has fought them successfully by thoroughly syringing the bushes with suds of carbolic-acid soap. In the open garden the bushes may be set in rows five feet apart, and four feet distant in the row. In obtaining gooseberries, ask for those varieties that do not mildew, such as Houghton's Seedling.

All kinds of fruit-trees and grape-vines may now be set out, even to better advantage than in the spring; and there is now no such pressure for time as will prevent its being done carefully. It may be safer farther north to put out stone fruits in spring, but that is a question for local authorities to decide. We are sufficiently utilitarian to advise the owners of small places to put out fruit-trees in the main, rather than those which are merely ornamental. If properly pruned and trained, fruit-trees are ornamental as well as useful. They are great fragrant bouquets in spring, and their laden boughs throughout the season suggest moral and religious lessons, good dinners, and spending money. Why should not all these things go together, good Doctor Theologicus?

As to varieties, if we are planting for home use, there should be a succession in time of ripening, with the main crop coming late, so that it will keep into the fall and winter. If we have the market mainly in view, then it is well to select more in view of the popular demand, learned from the market. We must also remember, that the list of highly recommended varieties is very large, and that some succeed admirably in one place, and not in another. We must therefore learn, by inquiry and observation, what kinds are best adapted to our locality.

We will see to it that we obtain only fair, straight, vigorous trees. No nursery-man shall palm off on us any others. Trees are like people. Each one has its own constitution, and some are dwarfed and weakly from the start. Sickly babies should have the tenderest care, but to feeble trees in their infancy, the Spartan law should apply. They should be destroyed.

Having obtained the trees, we will not put them in the ground like posts, but dig a fair round hole, twice as large and twice as deep as the roots seem to require. Many a sagacious man saves ten or fifteen minutes in setting out a tree, but loses half a dozen years in growth or bearing. Slip-shod work is usually economical after this style. In digging the hole, we will put all the good surface earth on one side, and the poor yellow subsoil on the other. The bottom of the hole will be filled up with good black soil, mixed with compost or *well-rotted* manure If a lot of bones can be thrown in also, their gradual decay will be of great benefit. Set the tree in the ground with roots well spread out, just as deeply as it stood before it was taken up

Sprinkle fine rich earth (never coarse manure) among and over the roots, so that they may have good ready material to draw on at once. Over the surface, the poor yellow soil from the bottom of the hole may be spread, and this covered with coarse manure as a mulch. Pour a pail of water around the tree, to settle the earth about its roots, and it is started like a boy with a good education. If it don't do well, it is its own fault. Of course, it wants looking after, from time to time, as we all do.

Grape-vines can be treated in the same general way, but we think that even the most hardy varieties had better be covered with earth the first winter, as a vine just set out cannot resist the cold like one long established. In choosing a spot for grape-vines, take one that is rather warm, dry, and with thorough drainage. Trees should have stakes at once, otherwise November winds will whip them to death; and three strong stakes should be driven over the little vine, or otherwise some careless foot may crush off the one or two buds on which your hopes may depend.

I have great faith in the raspberry as a profitable crop, and with me it has been next to the strawberry in value. The latter part of October is the best time to set them out. In spring there is apt to be delay, and the buds just above the roots that make the new canes are often so far started, that it is next to impossible to get the plants in the ground without breaking them off. If your plants are to consist of the Hudson River Antwerp, or some other tender and foreign variety, you can scarcely get your ground in too fine order. Not only must it be thoroughly enriched, but deep ploughing and careful cultivation is also required. If we are expecting to buy plants, it would be well, during the bearing season, to look around among those who have them for sale, and make our purchase of him whose vines show a tendency to great vigor and productiveness. For the same variety will look very differently, and really have marked diversities in different localities, and under varied treatment; and some growers' plants, from something unfavorable in soil or culture, become feeble in their constitution, and no amount of care can make them do so well as those from a thrifty stock. One great point of success is the continued selection of the strong and prolific. If the Clark and Philadelphia varieties are employed, the same high degree of fertility is not required, as they are naturally much more vigorous in their growth. But the same clean, careful culture should be practised with all kinds. Hard-baked soil, grass and weeds, will discourage the hardiest native varieties, and the cultivator will deserve nothing from his bushes but thorns.

We cannot recommend the Philadelphia variety, when better can be raised. It is true they are very hardy, and immense bearers, but the fruit is small, soft, and nearly all ripens at once, and if not all picked promptly, drops off. Still, on many soils other varieties do not succeed well, and on poor sandy ground this kind will do remarkably well. But put them in Washington Market alongside of the Antwerp, and they make a sorry show. For a local market, and when they can be sent to a city quickly without rough handling, the Clark is a very fine variety. The only trouble is, that they are very soft, and apt to mash down in carriage. But it is a hardy, kind, vigorous grower, and very prolific. They do not all ripen together either, and one has some leeway in getting them picked. Mine continue in bearing almost a month. There are some new varieties that are promising well

It would be well to make careful inquiries before setting out largely of any one kind, but for the home supply and a local market the Clark may be depended on; and if the Hudson River Antwerp does well in your locality, you need ask no better variety. My experience with the white varieties is, that they are too soft even for the local market, but they make a pretty change in the home garden. The Franconia (red) has proved an excellent berry with me, firm and productive. A new red variety called the Naomi is very highly spoken of. For field culture, raspberries should be set out four feet each way, so that the plough and cultivator can run between them.

The Philadelphia, Purple Cane, and Blackcap varieties need no protection in winter, and the same is also said of the Naomi. But even though it is claimed that the Clark and Franconia are perfectly hardy, I found it to pay to lay them down and cover with earth the same as the Antwerps. In the winter of '71-2 even the Philadelphias were badly killed, and it is my custom to bury this variety also. Last summer I visited a gentleman who had ten times as much ground in the Clark and Philadelphia varieties as I had, but my crop was ten times as large, I should think. Simply because my vines had been buried. Ten or twenty dollars spent in covering his vines would have given him five hundred dollars more in fruit.

In setting out your plants, cut them back to about six inches, so that all the strength of the root may go in producing new growth. Far more is lost than is gained by trying to get a crop the first year.

Blackberries may now be set out also. Their stronger habit of growth requires more space than raspberries, and, therefore, the rows should be at least six feet apart, and the plants stand four feet from each other in the row. The canes should be cut off about six inches above the ground, and the second season you may hope for a good crop. They do not by any means require as rich ground as the raspberry, and too high feeding would only injure them by stimulating too large a growth of immature wood. In our latitude the blackberry is so apt to winter-kill, that their cultivation is rather discouraging. If some perfectly hardy variety could be originated, it would be a great desideratum. The three varieties that I have tried, the Wilson, Lawton, and Kittatinny, all kill badly. The last two varieties are usually too strong and stocky to lay down and cover with earth as we do raspberries, but the more slender, trailing Wilson variety might be so treated without great difficulty. It has been my experience that blackberries require a light, thoroughly drained soil, so that the wood may ripen well before winter, while raspberries do better on a moist loam. A little shade is to the advantage of the latter also, and therefore it is well to set out standard pear-trees among them. The thorough cultivation required by the raspberries will greatly stimulate the growth of the trees, and their partial shade will be a benefit.

Cold frames should be ready the latter part of this month. Mine are made in the following simple, inexpensive way. A dry piece of ground is selected, which will be in no danger from melting snow and water, during the winter. The location should be sheltered from the north and west if possible. I sometimes excavate the soil two feet, throwing the good surface earth in one place, and the subsoil in another; then filling up the pit again, to the depth of one foot, with the best soil. Around the edge of this pit boards are placed, so as to form a simple box according in size to my sash. This box is made by nailing a wide board on the north side to firmly driven stakes, and a narrower one is arranged in the same way on the south side. Boards across the ends complete the rude, but effective appliance. The sash facing the south can now be laid on the boards when required, and the difference in width of the boards will give an inclination sufficient to carry off the water. When hurried, I have simply driven stakes in level ground, nailed the boards to them, and the work was done. But it is an additional protection to the plants to be twelve or eighteen inches below the surface of the ground. As I have picked up in our village old windows and sash of different sizes, I have made my boxes accordingly.

During the last ten days of October, I fill up these cold frames with lettuce, cabbage, and cauliflower plants, setting the last two named well in the ground—down to the leaves, so that no part of the stem is exposed. If the cabbage plants are rather small, they can be set from half to an inch apart in the rows, and the rows two inches apart; for growth is not aimed at now, but simply their preservation till spring.

I have always had the best success with lettuce, and seldom lose many plants. I put them as close as they can stand in rows three inches apart. Thus a small frame will winter over a great many. The ground must be pressed very firm about the roots, and kept so. Where it has tended to freeze and thaw during the winter and throw the roots out, I have found much advantage in filling up the spaces between the plants with dry sand.

At first these almost hardy vegetables will require no protection in the cold frames, but as freezing nights come on, the sash should be placed over them, and taken off during the day, and even during the winter they should be thoroughly aired in mild weather. As spring approaches the sash must be pushed down or taken off when the sun shines warmly, or the plants will be rendered tender, and premature growth induced. The earth should be heaped up around the outside of the boxes, as this renders them warmer and tighter. It is not necessary that the earth in these frames should be very rich, since they are used for storing rather than growing purposes. Still, I make the most of mine so, since early in spring I thin my lettuce-plants out by setting them in the open ground, or in frames prepared for forcing them. These are cold frames made in the fall, like those described above; but the earth in them is very rich, and designed to promote rapid growth. No plants are put in them in fall, and as winter approaches they are filled up with leaves, so that no frost can reach the soil. By the first of March the leaves can be thrown out, and you have rich, mellow ground in which lettuce-plants from the cold frames can be set out. They are then covered with glass, and by the end of the month are fit for market, while many of your neighbors have not as yet sown their seed.

All through the fall season, till the ground is frozen, much can be done in the way of improvement, and preparation for the following year, in the way of picking off stone, drainage, etc. Sometimes during the winter the water collects in parts of a field or garden, and does much harm. This can often be prevented by opening a small surface drain, from such localities, in November. All loam and clay lands are greatly benefited by deep ploughing, spading, or trenching in the fall. This very important work can often be continued even into December, and the gardener will find it greatly to his advantage to turn up every foot of land possible to the action of frost.

As winter approaches, we prune our tender raspberries, Wilson blackberries, and grapevines, then lay them down and cover with earth. Bury them well, or heavy rains will wash them out. Our strawberries should be tucked away under a good warm covering. I have usually employed stable manure, raking off only the coarsest part in the spring. In this way the plants are greatly stimulated as well as protected. But leaves, straw, or any litter will answer. Fruit trees may be carefully pruned at our leisure, by cutting back the too exuberant growth of new wood, and by trimming them into shapely appearance.

The closing scenes have come, and we are about ready to go into winter quarters. But after all this careful preparation for another season, we know that winter does not mean death to our garden. From the first white hoar-frost forward, autumn only brings to Nature rest and sleep.

In truth, Nature teaches man how to die, or rather how to provide for another life. There is much sentimental sighing over the falling leaves, fading flowers, and "winter's deadly breath."

"All that I see speaks to me of death," lamented a lachrymose moralist standing in a frost-bitten garden on a crisp, brilliant October day. This remark had been suggested by a shower of maple leaves, dropped around him by a sudden gust, that went ruthlessly through the grove, stripping the trees of their summer glory. And half the world sighs with him.

Why do they not note that the leaves are so rich and gay in coloring that they seem like rainbows falling in fragments. Why do they not see that every point where a leaf has parted from its spray, a bud has formed that will develop into other leaves, as large, green, and beautiful as were ever those now dropping away. Why should they not fall? Their work is done. They have reached their perfection. So far from assuming the sombre leaden hue of death before they change into other forms, they blush with joy, they crown themselves with gold, as if exulting over finished achievement. They are invested in the royal purple of victors, rather than the sad-colored hues of the vanquished.

But how about these frosted flowers that are in such sad contrast with their appearance a week ago? Even here death is more seeming than real. The frost did not fall till innumerable seeds were ripened, and this plant that looks so forlorn and dying, has a sturdy root, that, like a true, but unobtrusive friend, will see it through the "tight times" of frozen ground and icy nights.

While flourishing, blooming, fruiting, and having a good time generally in the summer sunshine, every plant in this garden, every shrub and tree on lawn or in grove, has at the same time been providing that it may live again. All the strength has not gone into one summer's growth. All the richness of ground and sap has not been expended in making a show for one brief season. In some wise, successful way, they have all the time been carrying forward the vital principle, that it might again be established under new and if possible more favorable auspices.

Shame on you, therefore, men and women of the world, who expend your whole strength on the passing hour on this first stage of the journey, this first crude phase of life, with no thought or provision for what is coming. Is this all your boasted reason—your high endowment does for you? Even the weeds of my garden do better, and while flourishing one season, at the same time see to it that their poor life may have a chance of flaunting under the blue skies and sunshine of another summer. Sad indeed would autumn be if your *death* took the place of Nature's change and sleep. Every bud on the leafless trees, every seed and root hiding in the snow-mantled earth, is a reproach to your narrow, earth-bounded life.

Were your gardens any the less luxuriant, beautiful, fruitful, last summer, because at the same time they developed the means of continuing so for all the future? And why should it take from the bloom of our lives, as we provide for their blossoming in a happier clime?

Every purple-tipped strawberry runner, every bud forming at the stem of the leaf, every ripening seed, should teach us that it is God's will that we should live and be happy in the future as well as in the present.

The frosts of autumn therefore do not mean death. They merely put Nature to rest when her proper bedtime comes, and winter soon after tucks her away under a fleecy blanket till the call of spring awakens.

But when disease attacks tree or plant, they may die even in the midst of spring showers and summer sunshine. It is sin, not death, that destroys man. All that death need mean is sleep, and a change for the better.

Sleep then, my garden! I know you will awaken, like some dear friends whose eyes I have seen closed, and their bodies, like the precious seed, covered deeply in the grave.

XIV.

GARDENING OVER A WINTER FIRE.

The holidays are past, and Santa Claus has either remembered us, or we were obliged to remember that we were Santa Claus. Snow and sleigh-riding have lost their novelty. We have been to town, read the new books, had the influenza, nearly finished our lecture course, and in brief have almost exhausted the proper things of the winter season. The days are growing longer, and often, something in their sunnier light and warmer breath reminds us of the friends in the garden, who are sleeping in their winter graves, still deep under the snow; but we know the time of resurrection is coming, when in robes new and rainbow-hued, they will rise from the earth into beautiful life.

The first hints of spring are subtle, delicate, but wonderfully suggestive. As you step out of your door some sunny morning the last of February, no matter how bleak and wintry the landscape may still appear, you feel in a vague, pleasurable way the influences of the opening season. There is a peculiar fragrance in the air, coming not from blossoms, for there are none, uncaused by budding vegetation, for as yet sleep rests on the pallid face of Nature. Not a bud has stirred, and the withered herbage is still buried deeply under the snow. And yet, by some strange alchemy, from some unknown source is this delicate perfume distilled. Do not the old farmers account for it when, on going out on such a morning, they snuff the air, and say:

" It smells like spring."

It is then spring's own peculiar and appropriate odor; and when we recognize it, we know that this most welcome season is near; just a certain fragrance assures us that a bunch of violets is not far off. The organization of the natural gardener is very susceptible to these influences, and when this impalpable aroma of spring first greets him, he has a solid satisfaction such as a stock dividend inspires in most men. He is allured by it to draw on his rubber boots and wade out into the snow-clad garden. But, after floundering around for a time with his pruning-knife, and having peeped into his cold frames—somewhat as the anxious mother occasionally looks into her crib and trundle-bed, where exuberant life is under the paralysis of sleep—he at last, chilled and shivering, gladly takes refuge in the warmest corner by the ruddy fire.

But the awakened garden spirit is strong upon him, and he cannot and will not resist its spells. Old numbers of the *American Agri-*

culturist or *Moore's Rural New Yorker* are dragged from some dusty hiding-place, and pored over with an interest that no plot in a novel can awaken. His limited library bearing on the garden will be drawn upon as he reads up on certain points, or seeks to learn the opinion of others as to the culture and value of certain crops.

And this leads us to say that a gardener's labors (if such you can call them) over a winter fire, are the most profitable in the year.

But little confidence does that campaign inspire which is carried forward on the hap-hazard principle; and strategy provided after dinner on hot afternoons will not answer for the main operations of the year. Therefore draw your desk or table to the easy-chair by the fireside, and with pen and paper elaborate your plans, so that when the season opens you will have nothing to do but carry them out with the utmost vigor. If taste and time permit, it is well to make maps of the garden, and indeed of one's entire place upon a certain scale, so that all may be accurately before the eye, rather than indefinitely present to memory. Then every tree will have its proper location, and it can be seen where others might be located. Ground already occupied can be so described, and you can carefully decide how you will plant the still open spaces. From garden manuals and papers, you can learn what crops are best suited to your soils, what modes of culture can be followed to greatest advantage. All now can be settled definitely for the best, but such wise deliberation would be impossible in the hurry of the opening season.

A clear, well-arranged plan always saves much time in all operations, but especially in a garden. In regard to culture and crops, there are such diversities of opinion and conflicting claims, that it is well to have something settled beforehand. Having resolved on some good methods, on selections that seem the best, push these right through, and if you have made mistakes and can see room for improvements, mark well just where, and make the changes for the better the following season. The man who in April or May is following the impulses of his own mind, bewildered by the variety of things that all need to be done at once seemingly, or who listens to a neighbor who leans over the fence and suggests, will probably have a strange jumble of a garden.

Then, in addition to the saving of time by having a plan, is the still greater saving of worry. A man who has a definite course marked out works with almost twice the ease and rapidity of one who does not know exactly what to do next. Worry wears much faster than work. It is like a shutter slamming back and forth to no purpose on a gusty day. Every spiteful bang is a jar and a wrench. Work is like well-oiled machinery running quietly in its grooves. Therefore, by careful plotting, careful reading and thought, and a well-digested plan, let us be prepared to work, not worry in our gardens, when spring opens. All this makes a pretty pastime for winter evenings, besides being eminently useful employment.

Agriculture offers scope for almost unlimited improvement. In no calling can skill and knowledge be made more effectual.

This knowledge is obtained, like that of any other subject, by thoughtful, judicious reading and observation, and by the most careful comparison of theories and broad generalizations of the facts of the garden. It will never do to apply to the garden the ancient mode of philosophy: that of first finding a theory that suits you, and then insisting that Nature shall conform to it. The good dame will probably do nothing of the kind, and then what is your theory worth? The Baconian system of facts first, and deductions afterwards, must apply here as elsewhere. But the gardener who remains ignorant of facts and makes no deductions, Nature justly frowns upon, and makes abundant deductions for him in the annual yield of his ground. I know that advocates of agricultural ignorance point to what they term "illiterate gardeners," and say:

"Look at what they accomplish without any reading, scientific or otherwise!"

Do they accomplish their success without knowledge? So many broad-minded persons (as they deem themselves) in good society, imagine that people must be well dressed, and read, in order to have knowledge. There are two ways of acquiring this: one from books, the other from things about which the books are written; and the latter is by far the best source of information, only it is school that "keeps in" a long time, and requires patient learners. It is in this that the "illiterate gardener," as you term him, has studied; but when you come to talk to him on his specialty, you may find that the illiteracy belongs to the questioner. If the kid-gloved theorist will go to work practically under Nature's instructions for a dozen years or more, he may find that though attending what may be termed a "dame's school," he will learn more than volumes can teach. Books aim to give, in brief, the slow teachings of experience, and as life is short, we avail ourselves of "short-cuts, and quick methods."

But the best knowledge is best gained by putting books and experience together, and letting one help the other Books broaden and liberalize, remove prejudices, and stimulate to higher attainment Facts, experience in the garden itself, corrects crude theories, and winnows out the chaff. But when it comes to skill, the "prentice hand" must acquire it mainly by practice. All the medical reading in the world would not make a good physician, though most essential in preparation; he must not only read about disease, but see it, treat it, and have experience in regard to it. But experience gives skill doubly fast, when careful reading and good abstract knowledge has prepared the way; and this preparation can best be made over the winter fire.

Then again, the spring catalogues are now arriving, and they are enough to give one a perfect fever over gardening. Lying before me is one that is a marvel of good taste and beauty, sent out by Mr. James Vick, of Rochester. In it advertising becomes a fine art. So suggestive and accurate are the engraving of vegetables, and especially the flowers, that we recognize old friends at a glance, and the latter stand out so clearly on the page, that it would seem that we could gather them into a bouquet. In sending out thousands of such catalogues, or rather pretty little volumes of one hundred and thirty-two pages, Mr. Vick may justly be regarded as a public benefactor, for they cannot fail to greatly increase the love for rural life; and they certainly impart much practical instruction in regard to it, while at the same time offering for sale the varied contents of the largest seed store in the world.

Looking as if it "meant business," R. H. Allen & Co.'s Catalogue, with its sober, solid appearance, catches my eye. It is an old friend, and has laid on my table every spring for ten years or more. Direct, simple, plainly indicating the best varieties among the many candidates for favor, it always inspires confidence. How often in the wane of winter I have looked through its pages, and marked the kinds I decided upon raising.

I can assure the ladies that the bliss of looking through the fashion-plates and ordering the spring styles, is not to be compared with the deliberation on the seeds you intend raising. Then only less welcome, because less familiar, are the catalogues of Peter Henderson, B. K. Bliss & Sons, Thorburn & Co., Bridgeman, Flemming, Landreth, Briggs & Brother, and others; and between them you are like a gourmand, who, instead of being invited to sit down to one feast, has placed before him a dozen banquets at the same time, and is bewildered how to choose.

As by a winter fire we turn over these dainty pages, what visions they conjure up to the imaginative amateur! "Conover's Colossal Asparagus!" How that sounds! but from brief trial I am coming to the conclusion that it does not sound too large. Farther on the eye is startled by "*Egyptian Blood——!*" oh! "Egyptian blood turnip Beet, the earliest variety grown," and we breathe freer. What names they give these innocent useful vegetables! Why "Egyptian Blood"? Who wants so sanguinary an association while weeding his early beets? Now here is something sensible: "Large Flat Dutch Cabbage." That is very appropriate. The carrot list commences badly. "The Early Horn!" I hope none of my readers take it, early or late. Then here is "Carter's Incomparable Dwarf Dark Crimson Celery." Such a name as that certainly requires a carter. "Early Russian" or "Rush-in," as it is generally pronounced, is a good name for a fast cucumber, but I protest against "Blue Peter Pea." I told you the onion was irrepressible and supreme in every age; for see, they have named the last variety discovered,

"New Queen," and I promise you she will maintain her *rank* when so many of her degenerate sisters are losing theirs. Other queens may frantically sway their sceptres in vain, but a breath from her will cause many to grow sick and faint. Long live the new Queen—onion. For the sake of our Democratic friends, I will add that she is described as having a "white skin." Here is something called Scorzonera. The idea of asking your youngest child if he would take some of that for dinner! We come next to a squash called "Hubbard," probably in honor of the good old lady of that name, in hopes that her "cupboard" will never be "bare" of the delicious pies it makes. Strange! here is one called the "Boston Marrow." The profanity of suggesting in faintest allusion that the marrow of Boston enters in a squash! We hardly know what we are coming to in the way of Tomatoes. Every year there are several novelties so far superior (according to the catalogues) to anything else known, that it would seem perfection might be reached in this vegetable, if nothing else earthy. Two or three years ago, we had a variety named General Grant, indicating that all competitors were vanquished. We bought General Grant, sowed it, hoed it, and ate it, and were satisfied. General Grant didn't disappoint us—never. It was a good tomato, *solid* all the way through; and though not so large as some others, was very prolific. We hoped to "have peace" on the tomato question. But so far from being satisfied, like the people, with the great namesake for eight years, the seed-growers all proved Liberal Republicans on the tomato question, and every spring new candidates are pressed upon us. And now, Mr. "Smith" has sent out a novelty that renders it almost impossible to wait till next July before seeing the wonder in fruit. The only thing that can be done at present is to buy the seeds at twenty-five cents per half dozen or so

But as far as names are concerned, the vegetables get off very well. It is when we turn to the flowers that our deepest sympathies are aroused. Here is a poor little plant, six inches high at the best, overwhelmed with " Kaulfussia amelloides atroviolacea." What a wrong is done to the pretty modest little flower! I would not put this name on a label over the seed, for it would never dare come up. Imagine a lisping young lady asking a bashful young man to go into the garden and make her a bouquet of " Agrostemma," " Asperula azurea setosa," " Dianthus Heddewigii flore pleno atropurpureus," " Phlox Drummondii Radowitzii Kermesina striata," " Helichrysum brachyrrhinchum," and a few more pretty little blossoms. And yet, Mr. Vick and others gravely offer these varieties, and a host of other unpronounceables, for our modest flower-borders, stating that they are "desirable for cutting." Their names are certainly, and might be cut back indefinitely. The winter fire would burn out, and spring come and go, before we could master the cabala of the floral catalogues. I pounce down on the Pansies, Asters, and like old friends, who have not put on such airs in the way of names, that one does not know them. But they, too, have caught the infection, and are coming on like some boys I used to know, who are getting " D. D." and " Esq." to their names, and are no longer known as " Tom " or " Hal."

But the evening wanes, our eyes grow weary, our minds confused between the conflicting claims of seeds, each one with a stronger or longer title to attention than its fellow. We wish we had a hundred acres, and a dozen gar‑ deners, and could plant each kind in rows as long as their names, and thus find out for certain which were really the best.

At last we sweep books and seductive catalogues aside, lift our feet on the fender, and lean back in our easy-chair. Falling into a dreamy state, we conjure up some sort of an ideal Eden in which fancy is head gardener, and wishes wait to do its bidding. Having reached the strawberry-bed in our imaginary scene, we rest satisfied, and drop off into a doze—to awake an hour later, chilled and shivering. The winter fire has gone out, and we find a feather, rather than a strawberry-bed, is the proper thing.

"The time of the singing of birds is come."

A brass band banging away after bedtime, or in ancient times the voice of a Troubadour twanging a guitar under a window at some unseasonable hour—often mistaken on first awakening no doubt for a cat—these are perhaps the traditional ideas of a serenade. But what language can portray your feelings when you are awakened some mild morning in March by the wild minstrelsy of a party of robins and bluebirds that, coming from you know not where, have taken possession of your garden. The long oppressive silence of winter is broken, and now we shall have trills, solos, duetts, and choruses that can only be imitated in the Academy of Music.

Song is the first crop I obtain from my garden, and one of the best. The robins know I am a friend of theirs in spite of their taste for early strawberries and cherries, and when I am at work they are very sociable and familiar. One or two will light on raspberry stakes near, and sing and twitter almost as incessantly and intelligently as the children in their play-house under the great oak tree. And yet the robin's first mellow whistle in spring is a clarion call to duty, the opening note of the campaign.

The making of a hot-bed may perhaps be regarded as the first labor to be performed. Its size will depend somewhat on that of your garden, and whether you intend raising plants for sale.

The frame or box on which your sash are to rest should be made more carefully than that of the mere cold frame, for the hot-bed is designed for growth instead of storage. The sash should run in grooves, and the boards overlap, so that no cold air can find access when it is closed. Light pine shutters, straw mats, or old carpet should be provided to render it still more secure from the cold. The pits over which the frames and sash are placed should be made in the fall, and filled up with leaves as before described. At any time from the first to the middle of March, these leaves can be thrown out, but kept dry as possible, and fresh manure from the horse stable mixed with them in equal proportions, and all well shaken together in a compact conical heap. In a few days it will commence heating, as can be seen from the vapor thrown off. It should then be shaken out and piled up again, and after two or three days a second fermentation will take place, and now it can be placed evenly and tramped down in the bottom of the pit to the depth of two and a half feet, and seven inches of soil spread over it. This brings the surface about two feet from the glass. Before sowing the seeds it is better to wait three or four days, as the manure may heat so violently that it would destroy the tender germs. When a thermometer placed in the soil would recede to eighty-five, then seed can be sown. The earth in the beds should be very fine and rich, and may be kept in some cellar, or more conveniently in a cold frame covered with leaves. Early cabbage, cauliflower, and lettuce should be sown first. The seed of pansies, petunias, phlox, asters, ten weeks' stock, and all the Dianthus tribe can be sown also. I do not think it well, usually, to plant tomatoes, pepper, and egg-plant seed before the 20th of March, as they are so impatient of cold. And these last should be planted in one end of the hot-bed by themselves, as they need less airing, and more covering than their hardier neighbors. Great care must be exercised in preventing the plants from becoming chilled cold nights and wintry days, and even more vigilance is required in seeing that they are properly aired and hardened in their growth. By leaving the sash closed with a hot morning sun shining on them, I have seen an entire bed ruined in an hour. And from want of proper airing and hardening, the plants in very many hot-beds are so tende and spindling as to be almost worthless. When set in the open ground they wilt right down. In the hands of a careful gardener who can give it his own supervision, and who carefully transfers the tender plants from it to a cold frame, and from thence to the open ground, a hot-bed is very useful. But in our March weather it requires considerable judgment and constant watchfulness. To tell the truth, I make little use of them, save for forcing lettuce in March. For this purpose I find them excellent, and have lettuce growing nicely now, the last of February, though the thermometer has marked six below zero during the present week.

As I have shown, I winter over in cold frames hardy vegetables; and even for raising the tender ones in spring, I prefer the ordinary cold frame, with ground made fine and very rich, sowing the seed of hardy plants early in March, and of the tender ones the first of April, and having no other heat than that of the sun on the glass. My tomato plants so raised may not be so large as those from a hot-bed, but they are hardy, stocky, and go right ahead, when set in the open ground. My friend Mr. Skene often supplements my home supply most liberally, he being furnished the means and possessing the skill to do everything in the best possible way.

In many localities the gardeners can dispose of a large number of surplus plants if carefully grown, and of varieties that they can recommend. I have not done very much in this way, as I have not had the conveniences; but in '71, one thousand five hundred and twenty-eight tomato plants were sold for sixteen dollars and seventy-three cents; while thirteen dollars and twenty cents were received for cabbage and cauliflower plants, and a much larger sum for the same in '72.

With the first of March commences the utmost activity with the cold frames. The sun has now gained such power, that so hardy a vegetable as lettuce will commence growing under glass. The leaves are therefore thrown out of the frames, and the soil, made very rich and fine last fall, is now heated up by keeping the sash on tightly a few days, and then set out in plants which we have been keeping in the storage frames. As soon as these are thus emptied, they are forked over, enriched, and filled with plants for heading also. By the middle of the month the sash can be taken off the storage frames altogether, and all your glass, save that used in starting new seeds, employed in forcing lettuce and radishes for market. Even in this winter of '73, the severest we have ever known, I expect to carry safely through eight thousand plants, and by March 15th to have at least two thousand set out for heading in cold frames. On the 22d of February I had two hundred and fifty growing finely As soon as the frost is out, a warm, sheltered place in the open garden can be filled with the hardy lettuce plants from the cold frames, and I have had these mature for market in May. Cabbage and cauliflower wintered over can also be set out in the open garden as soon as the ground can be worked. In forcing lettuce, great watchfulness is required. Of course, you want to keep up the utmost degree of heat without injuring the plants, as this brings them into market sooner. But too great heat may damage if not spoil your crop. The danger increases as the leaves in their growth approach the glass. Whenever the sun shines, it is safer to push the sash down a little, even early in the morning, and give an increasing amount of outer air as the sun grows higher. In the afternoon gradually push the sash up, and before there is any chill close up tightly. On cold, cloudy, windy days the sash need not be touched. If there should come warm rains, strip the sash off altogether; and if not, sprinkle often tepid water, as this greatly hastens the growth.

The spring of '71 was very mild and open, and I had lettuce under glass fit for use the 17th of March. It was not full grown by any means, but pretty fairly so, and by the 24th it was selling rapidly. My sales for that season amounted to sixty-one dollars—averaging about four cents a head. In the spring of '72 my lettuce sold for ninety-one dollars and eighty-two cents. I have a third more glass in '73 than ever before, and hope for correspondingly large receipts. After the first of June the demand for this vegetable is not worth mentioning, and the main crop is forced under glass.

To a limited extent I have found parsnips and salsify or oyster plant profitable crops. The earlier the seed is sown after the frost is out of the ground, the better; the salsify in rows one foot apart, and plants three inches in the row; parsnips in rows fifteen inches apart, and thinned out so as to stand four inches from each other. The soil where they are grown should be made rich and deep, and good clean cultivation will insure a large crop. In November, what are needed for winter can be dug, put in barrels, and covered with damp earth, to keep them from wilting; then stored in a cool cellar. But the majority of the roots can be left in the open ground till spring, for freezing does them good. As soon as frost is out, they can be dug as required; and as vegetables are so scarce in March and April, they usually find a ready sale. In the spring of '71 I had three and a quarter bushels of parsnips to dispose of, but for these, sold in small quantities, Thomas received six dollars and eighty-eight cents. The salsify was sold in bunches, ten or twelve roots in a bunch, and seven dollars and eighteen cents were obtained for seventy-seven bunches. Where the latter vegetable is appreciated and meets with ready sale, it can be made very profitable. The bulk of the crop should be so stored that it can be sold during the winter. If placed in a cellar, it is very apt to wilt and become worthless, and therefore should be stored out of doors. One simple way of doing this is to cut a trench one foot in depth and width, through some dry, well-drained ground, and then pack the roots in this, standing as they grew. The earth may be gathered slightly over them, so that the green tops will partially show through it. They should not be so stored till just before severe freezing weather commences, and they can be so covered with leaves and straw as to be accessible any time during the winter. If parsnips or other roots are raised in large quantities, they had better be stored in pits out of doors, as most cellars, either from heat or dryness, cause them to decay or wilt.

Once more I will return to the onion, and then its delicate aroma shall no longer breathe through these pages. But since it is one of the most profitable crops of the garden, and can be put in the ground even before the frost is out in the spring, it must find mention here again. The beds that have been wintered over should be gradually but *early* uncovered. The plants are hardy to the cold, but the tops are apt to smother and decay if anything rests closely on them when the weather grows mild. They will commence growing as soon as the frost gives them the slightest chance, and in '71 I had them fit for market by March 25th. When I have not a sufficient number started the previous fall, I obtain a very early supply for market by putting out refuse and sprouted onions, purchased for a trifle at the stores. No matter how large or how far gone they are, if the germ is sound. If the sprouts are long and spindling, cut them off, about an inch above the bulb. Set them out in very rich ground, as soon as you have even three inches of soil above the frost. I have them put in rows, six inches apart, and close enough to touch each other. They will commence growing at once, and in about four weeks will be ready for market. Their large green tops, while young and tender, are highly valued by those who are not much in the kissing line. Thomas says that he does not sell many to young ladies. But from the demand, I should judge that kissing is but a limited source of happiness, while onions are quite the reverse; so wishing to add as largely as possible to the enjoyment of the world, I plant much of my garden in this secret of human joy. A very eminent Divine once told me, that this sacred vegetable contributed greatly to the increase and nourishment of the brain. May not this account for the general demand for it? People oppressed by the need of brains instinctively turn to a source of supply. But I can assure the prospective gardener, whether he has need of brains or not, if he has need of cash, here is a good way of supplying it. The earlier in spring he puts out his "sets," and "top onions," or sows the seed, the better; for those started first seem to do the best. In '71, one thousand eight hundred and sixty-five bunches were sold in their green state for ninety-two dollars and forty-four cents. Also six bushels and eleven quarts, realizing sixteen dollars and ninety cents. In addition, four and one-half bushels of sets, or little onions for seed, were sold for twenty-three dollars and sixty-two cents. In summing up, therefore, even if the onion has not done much for me in the way of brains, I cannot complain.

Radishes, also, demand attention as early as possible in the market garden. I find them a profitable crop in the cold frame, and expect to sow quite a large space in this way, while the snow averages two feet in depth over the garden. By the 10th of April, they ought to be ready for market. They can be sown under glass in rows five inches apart, and the ground should be very fine and rich. I also aim to sow my main crop out of doors, in March if possible, on warm, light soil; and I find that it pays to fill up the shallow drills in which the seed is sown, with some black, well-rotted manure. This draws the sun, and stimulates rapid growth; and unless a radish grows quickly, it is worthless. It is rather an uncertain crop, as it has serious enemies to contend with. In the first place, as soon as it shows itself above the ground, a little black beetle or flea attacks it, and will often destroy first plantings in a few hours. I have tried soot and other things, but have found no remedy so effective as little chickens. Put a coop on each side of your radish bed, and let the little chicks run over it, and they will soon clean it thoroughly of the pest. This same black flea will attack early turnips, cabbage, and indeed almost anything green early in the season; and where I have but one or two flocks of chickens, I have Thomas move them every night, to some point where the "wicked flea" is specially destructive, and in the morning the devourers are themselves devoured. This is in accordance with Nature's theory, that one thing should eat another thing, and so keep the ratio of existence nicely adjusted. That the theory may be proved correct in its last analysis, men and women in America do not need cannibals, for care and worry do the work much more effectually.

Another and still more formidable difficulty, in radish cultivation, is a little white worm that attacks the growing root. The only remedy seems to be to employ new or different soil every year, making it so rich as to secure such a rapid growth that the worm has no time for its depredations. But I lose a great many in this way every season. Besides, there is a great difference in radish seed, especially that of the " Long Scarlet Short Top," which often proves all top. I have found great differences in seed of the same name, some tending to produce large roots promptly, and some tending never to produce them. I do not think that seedsmen can always know of these differences themselves. I buy my seed in small packages of several dealers, and when I have a package producing the best and earliest, purchase largely of that. If kept in a cool, dry place, the seed will remain good for several seasons, as it retains its vitality for five years.

My sales in '71 were not as large as usual, but amounted to nine hundred and sixteen bunches, realizing thirty-five dollars and nine cents. I have grown them between beets and other vegetables, but find that, unless you have a prompt sale for them the day they are ready, they are apt, by remaining a few days, to so injure the crops they are grown with as to be unprofitable. In a small local market you cannot sell out at once. With your best management, a week or so after you have radishes every one with a small garden has them also, and the demand drops off rapidly. I sow my earliest beds where I shall put egg-plants, tomatoes, and such late tender vegetables, and they are out of the way in time for these to be set out in May. The first week in April I also have hills for melons, cucumbers, etc., formed about four feet apart, by mixing a shovel or two of light well-rotted manure with the soil and rounding it up for the sun to warm and dry out. The seed for the hills is not planted till from fifth to the tenth of May, but the ground between the hills can be sown thickly with radishes, and long before the melon or other vines want the space, they are out of the way. The earliest, and those grown in cold frames, will bring five cents per bunch; but when they fall below two cents, they do not pay, sold in small quantities.

March brings many and varied labors in the garden. Grape-vines should be trimmed if they were not last fall, and the pruning-knife should be busy generally. Tools, seeds, plants, trees, should be ready, or ordered, so that when good weather fairly opens, not a moment need be lost.

When we shall get to work in the open ground

March, '73, it is hard to say. Now, at the opening of the month, snow covers the ground to the depth of two feet, and the title of one of Bulwer's novels, slightly changed, might well be addressed to Nature. "What *will*" she "do with it" between now and April 1st? March promises to maintain its proverbial bad character; and yet this month, so universally inveighed against, is to me one of the most fascinating. Its darkest days are full of hope and the knowledge of the near approach of spring. We laugh at winter's gloomiest frowns, since the old tyrant cannot long maintain them, and must soon abdicate in favor of a gentler sovereign. Already spring, like a young queen consort, tempers his harshness, and soon she will occupy the throne alone. Increasingly often there are bright, warm, suggestive days when the decrepit tyrant cannot appear, and she, unchecked, sways the sceptre, all sweetness, grace, and benignity.

Or to change the figure, this season, so uncertain and variable, now smiling and gentle, now harsh and forbidding, reminds one of coy, cold beauty about to yield to love's suit in spite of herself. She tries, but cannot maintain her frowns, for love softens her heart like the subtle south wind relaxing the frozen earth. Though her moods are abrupt and trying in their changes they are followed by remorseful tears, just as rain one day seeks to banish the frost and snow of the preceding. Her temper is often high and uncertain, her words a little sharp and blustering, like March winds; but wait patiently till all has blown over, and see how softly and sweetly she will smile on you. But don't presume; don't felicitate yourself too highly; there will probably be a change. Patient wooing and waiting shall be well rewarded by the tearful penitence and sunny smiles of April, and warmer affection of May and June.

XV.

APRIL

" Bestir, bestir."

No time for sentiment now, for Nature is not only thoroughly awake, but up and busy, and we shall do well if we keep pace with her. Seemingly, there are a dozen things to be done at once, these mild April days, but one thing at a time is the secret of progress, with some modification. Where you have several in help, one or two can often work to better advantage at a certain task than half a dozen, and if you employ boys, the less they help each other the more they accomplish.

In the first place, tie up your grape-vines; don't leave them sprawling on the ground till the buds start. In this respect my words have all the authority belonging to those of a certain temperance lecturer, who, in order to be graphic and forcible, occasionally got drunk, that he might speak from experience.

Fruit-trees and grape-vines can now again be set out, and the earlier it is done the better. This is specially true in regard to raspberries, or else the buds or germs that are to make the bearing canes for another season will be so far started as to render it impossible to prevent their breaking off. If a full supply of all kinds of fruit were not put out the preceding fall, we would urge that it be done in spring, and if done early and carefully, and the ground kept mulched and moist around the plants and trees during the hot dry weather, the gardener will have no cause to complain.

For certainty of success there is no time for putting out strawberry plants like April. If done early in the month, with ordinary care, they are sure to grow. I aim to set out one or two new beds every spring. When you are buying new and expensive varieties this is the time, by all means.

It is a pleasure and often a source of profit to try a few of the novelties, and some extraordinary ones (on paper) are offered for '73 (vide catalogues and advertisements). Certain new kinds are offered at the modest sum of fifty cents each, and one or two of these I shall try. A single plant is all you want. From that you can obtain fifty that will bear the following season, and so in a small way can thoroughly test the value of the variety. If it is what you want, you can raise enough new plants from the fifty during the second summer to set out all you wish, and have many to spare. It is therefore interesting to try in this inexpensive manner some of the large, new, highly recommended kinds, as among them you may find something just adapted to your soil and locality. But in setting out largely, obtain some well-known variety, that your neighbors recommend from trial. Prepare and enrich your ground thoroughly, and if pressed for room, the spaces of two feet between the strawberry rows can be occupied by radishes, lettuce, onion sets, or spring-sown spinach. Last spring I had early beets sown between the rows of a strawberry-bed. The beets were marketed in June and July, and by fall the strawberry rows were closely filled with new strong plants, which promise a very large crop this year. Still, where ground is plenty, cultivation is more easy and rapid when everything is grown by itself, with wide spaces between, and only very rich soil, with careful culture, will bear crowding.

Asparagus and rhubarb roots should also be set out as early as possible in April. As the former may remain in bearing on the same ground for twenty-five or thirty years, the most careful preparation is required, and yet we do not think there is any need of going to the great expense that many indulge in. If a small bed is to be made in a garden, let it be trenched and enriched to the depth of two feet. In the spring of '72 I put out quite a large bed of Conover's colossal asparagus. I obtained the roots of R. H. Allen & Co., and do not remember whether they were one or two years old, but they were of fair size and in good order. I put them out in some of my best ground, in the following simple way: Commencing at one end of the bed that had been well prepared, my gardener opened a trench about fourteen inches deep and slightly slanting on one side. The plants were then leaned against the slanting side, one foot apart from each other, and enough good soil thrown around to partially cover and keep them in their place, and a small shovel of rotted manure given to each plant. Stepping back two feet, another trench was opened, and the plants treated in the same manner, and in this way the entire bed was soon planted, and the soil over the plants (which were covered about four inches) was left smooth and untramped. Although a fine crop of beets was raised between these rows, the asparagus made a very vigorous growth, and if I should decide to cut it the second year from planting (as I probably shall, since it is on leased land), there will be a fair crop. When the very best results are aimed at, and the purpose is to maintain the bed in good productiveness as long as possible, it is best not to cut the young asparagus shoots till the third year.

All the cultivation required is to keep the ground clean and mellow during the summer. In field culture the rows had better be three feet apart, so that a cultivator can run between them. In the fall the bed should be mowed off, and those tops that are not full of seed make an excellent covering for such hardy plants as require but slight protection. Cover the bed if small, or the rows if large, with three inches of manure, before hard freezing weather commences in fall, and your asparagus so treated will not fail to give good satisfaction. It is a vegetable that always sells, and I doubt if the market ever will be overstocked.

Perhaps there is no crop that the possessor of a garden near a small local market could grow with greater prospects of success than this, if he has the patience to put it out in the right way and take good care of it. Being in itself such a favorite, and coming when there is so little variety for the table, it always sells high. It will adapt itself to any soil that is well enriched and kept so, and when treated in accordance with its nature—that is, given ground where it grows with its native vigor—it makes a large return. In its wild state it flourishes along the coast in certain regions of Europe and Asia, and since its introduction to this country, has found its way in some instances to the beaches and marshes of our own shores. Hints from its history and taste should be taken, and we should seek to give it a soil suited to its peculiar habit. If we have on our places a sandy alluvial piece of ground and will deepen and enrich it, we would have no trouble in raising large paying crops of asparagus. A swamp that can be thoroughly drained so that no water would stand at any time of the year, would also make a fine place for a late crop. Indeed, great advantage would be secured by such variety of soil as would give a succession. Some very warm location with a light sandy soil might be selected for the early growth, and a cooler, moister soil for the main crop. Of course the earliest would bring, in most places, by far the largest price. But I find that in my local market the fluctuations of price are not very great. I cannot, to any extent, reach the New York fancy retail mark, even for articles sold in this way, nor do they often fall below a fair paying return. I am well satisfied that a large bed of asparagus would give a profitable crop that could be depended on every year. One naturally hesitates in putting out a crop of this character on leased ground. It is the same as setting out grape-vines, and you cannot expect much return before the third year. And yet I have done this, believing that but one or two crops of so fine a vegetable would repay all trouble. But if one has bought a place to sell again, and therefore their stay may be transient or at least uncertain, we would advise them to put out a bed by all means. One good crop would nearly if not quite compensate for outlay, and an asparagus bed ought to be regarded as a permanent improvement like an orchard, and should add to the value of a place.

Those of us whose gardens are not near the coast, will find salt very beneficial to our asparagus. Two pounds to the square yard can be scattered over the ground very early in spring, as soon as the ground is forked over, and the rain will wash it down. While helping the vegetable, it will disgust the bugs, worms, and weeds generally, they having no sympathy with the "salt of the earth."

But with rhubarb a small local market can easily be more than supplied. I have about twice as much as we need, but as it takes up but little room, and requires not a great deal of attention, I let it grow, intending to try to increase the demand by selling it cheaply.

As this vegetable also stands a number of

years on the same ground, thorough preparation should be made for it. The soil cannot be made too rich, and every spring it must be abundantly stimulated; and this, with keeping it free from weeds, is all that is required. I have Thomas put a good shovel of manure on the crown of every plant in November, and this keeps them warm, and starts them early in spring. The ground should be dug around them as soon as the frost is out.

The earlier new plants are set out the better. They can be procured at any seed store, and, for a local market, it is best to order the largest variety, even if it is a little later. The plants should be set so that the crown, or bud, is barely under ground. Make the rows four feet apart, and let the roots stand three feet from each other in the row. Its time of readiness for market will vary with the season. In '71 my sales commenced April 28th, and for two hundred and seventeen bunches, twenty dollars and fifty cents were received; while in '72, it was May 8th before any were sold; but the crop was larger and better. If speculators in sugar would only send all families in the country a dozen or more rhubarb plants, there is no telling what fortunes might be made. I make this saccharine suggestion to avert any charge of acidity of style; but if this hint is followed, and fortunes are made, I shall expect my share, and no investigations.

Quinces can now be set out also to good advantage. Instead of letting them grow into scraggly bushes, it is much better to prune them into shapely pyramidal trees (but please do not inquire into my practice). Currant and gooseberry cuttings can still be put out, as directed, in the fall, or the earth heaped up about those designed for division into new plants, but it must be done early.

Those who live in Virginia, and South, should set out their fig-trees now. When chaplain at Fortress Monroe, I raised them with the same ease that we do currants here; and the fruit is such a favorite one with me, that I shall try them in our latitude this spring, laying them down and burying them like raspberries in the fall.

I raise mainly the dwarf varieties of peas, and having tried several, I have at last settled down on two varieties—the "Tom Thumb" for earliest crop, and McLean's Little Gem for second. The first is very hardy, and can be planted as soon as the frost is out of the ground—the earlier the better. It grows about eight inches high, and if not planted too closely in the row is very prolific. I have had them and the tall Marrowfat growing at the same time in my garden. and found that a vine of the Tom Thumb produced as many pods as a vine of the tall variety standing between four and five feet high. The rows of Tom Thumb can be planted one foot apart, the others four feet, and require brush at that. But to get a paying crop from the dwarfs they must be planted *early* on very rich soil. I find it pays well to drill in well-rotted manure with the seed. McLean's Little Gems are not quite so hardy, and should not be planted till after the soil becomes a little warmer and drier. When ground is scarce and valuable, as with me, I find these dwarf varieties pay much the best, as I can plant them between other crops, such as raspberries, sweet corn, lima beans, cucumbers, etc. The Tom Thumb, if sown very early, will mature about the 20th of June in our region, and as the pods all fill out at once the vines can be pulled up as they are picked, and thus they are out of the way of the crops they were growing between. I always fill up my tomato ground this way the last of March or first of April. One of the simplest methods is to open a double row three and a half feet apart. This double row consists of two shallow trenches three or four inches deep and five inches apart. In these the peas are sown so as to stand about an inch from each other, and slightly covered. If then black, well-rotted manure is scattered over them, it will draw the sun and greatly stimulate their growth. By the 10th of May, tomato plants can be set out between these double rows, and one crop will not interfere with the other, for long before the tomatoes cover the ground, the peas will be gathered and sold. Of course this will only pay in small gardens where cultivation with a plough is not practised. I also aimed by planting McLean's Little Gems, and some later kinds, to have a succession of crops; and as they were mostly sold in small quantities to those who valued quality, eighteen bushels and fourteen quarts brought the large sum of forty-three dollars and sixty cents. For field culture, where ground is plenty, and not very rich, the tall kinds, like Dan O'Burk, McLean's Advancer, and Champion of England, are doubtless the best. But don't hire your men to pick them by the day. I gave an Irishman twelve shillings last summer to pick about fifty cents' worth of peas.

He would be little better than a heathen (agriculturally) who raised no peas for home supply; but we have strong doubts as to the profitableness of this vegetable for market. I think you can raise more strawberries to the acre than you can peas. You can pick a bushel of the fruit as soon, and the latter will bring from six to ten dollars a bushel, while for the former you often cannot get one dollar. For a small local market it will pay well to plant the dwarfs between other crops, thus making your ground do double duty. Or growing the best and largest kinds, like the Champion of England, giving them brush and extra care, will compensate the gardener, if he is not limited in land, and can obtain a fair price through the season. For the choice wrinkled varieties, picked young and deliciously fresh, people ought to be willing to pay double price. With the majority who buy at market, however, a peck of peas is a peck of peas, whether it came from Long Island or Norfolk a week ago, or that morning from a neighboring garden, and price alone is considered.

There is no use of trying to grow this vegetable on a large scale, unless you are near some village, and can employ a dozen pickers or more, the day it is ready. The pods will become unsalable almost as soon as small fruit if left on the vines, and the difference of one day in the market price may be that of utter loss instead of good profit. In our region very early and very late crops sell for the largest sums.

For further pea-ticulars, see Mr. Burr's valuable book, in which he reduces one hundred and sixty-two varieties named to *only* seventy-three, and these he describes.

XVI.

GRAFTING, OR HORTICULTURAL CONVERSION.

During the first warm still days of this month, as soon as the buds begin to swell, grafting should be performed. The operation is neither so agreeable nor successful on cold, windy days. This simple but very useful labor of spring can be learned by once witnessing it, better than from any description; and in every locality there are adepts in the art, who will either do the work or show the amateur how to perform it himself, which is better. On almost every place there are vigorous young trees grown from chance seed, but this wild or natural fruit is of but little value. By a few grafts we can put all this native vigor of growth into some of the most approved luscious varieties. Why cannot reformers and teachers work more on this principle? With multitudes, repression seems the favorite method of getting the world right "Thou shalt not" enact government. "It is not proper," cries society with elevated eyebrows. "You mustn't do this, don't do that," constantly falls on the little children's ears; and preaching consists more largely in telling men what they ought not to do, than in what they may and should do. Nice little boys and girls, that were started rightly from the first, and had grace "budded in" with their mother's milk, get along very well. They go out into the world like trees from the rows in the nursery, straight, pruned, labelled, and warranted, though often a little weakly. Still they have much to be thankful for, and all they have to do is to grow as they have been directed. But society is full of boys and girls that have come up on "their own hook," to use their own vernacular; just as we find wild apple, cherry, and pear trees growing along fences, in thickets and all sorts of unexpected places.

As a general thing, these fortuitous youth are morally not elected or highly favored, and when mature enough to bear the fruit of characteristic deeds, we say:

The less of that kind the better.

But what shall we do with them? Repression, cutting back, only increases their wild growth. To be sure we can dig them out, root and branch, and destroy them; and this was society's ancient course with those unruly members who would not grow morally, mentally, and religiously in the narrow little mould of the times. But this will not answer now, much as some good people would like to try it..

But what shall we do? Nature teaches us.

A few feet away from my parsonage-door, a

young cherry sapling took a notion to grow. Nobody planted it, nobody wanted it there. It was rather in the way, and how it managed to escape being trampled down or cut down, is a mystery akin to that of the life and vigor of some children against whom everything seems to conspire. Before I realized it, there was flourishing right before my door a tall, shapely sapling, but in a state of nature rather than one of grace, and commencing to bear villanously small and bitter fruit.

Something must be done. To let it grow on its rampant style, and destroy with its baneful shade two saintly little pear-trees standing near, would not answer. To dig it out would be a mean, cowardly way of meeting the question, besides being unscriptural. Indeed, my reputation as a clergyman was at stake. If I could not convert this little horticultural sinner growing right under my nose, what impression could

I hope to make on the unregenerate world at large?

Not far off, there was a tree of large, splendid ox-hearts. Cutting a scion or twig, four inches long, of the preceding summer's growth, from this, I carefully grafted the main stem of the child of nature; but made it a point to leave a few little branches on which the young blood (sap, I should say) could expend some of its superabundant vitality.

Here is another point where reformers bring in their everlasting repression. Even when they give some irrepressible young sinner good wholesome work to do, they insist on his doing that and nothing else. It is the same as if they required that the old life of the tree should cease at once, and every drop of sap go into the graft. It can't do it, and it won't. Leave some little branches to grow with the graft a year or so, gradually pruning them out, and throwing the whole strength into the increasing graft. The tree will submit kindly to this considerate treatment, though it will not stand a square cut from sinner to saint, but right through its bark, everywhere will throw out buds of the old stock with resentful frequency and power. I do not know how it is with my brethren, but I find the same principle holds good in the parish.

At any rate, this treatment was most successful on the subject described, and I gradually induced all its abounding vigor to go into the graft alone, and last summer it bore some of the largest, finest cherries I ever saw.

This suggests a very serious blunder I once made, while seeking to bring about a certain horticultural reformation. In this case the tree was past the sapling stage, and might be described in its early prime, reminding one of a young man at the age of twenty-five.

Indeed, it did remind me of several young

men, and young ladies too, that I knew of, who were well educated, abounding in health and strength, but whose lives bid fair to be as useless as that of my cherry-tree. Those of us who regard present existence as something more than a "play spell," often look very wistfully and regretfully on the waste of human vitality around us. The world seems to us like a garden that might be abundantly productive of fruits so precious, that angels would store them in heavenly garners; and yet it is ready to perish for lack of weeding and cultivation.

So it appeared to the Divine Husbandman, and He commands all to labor in His vineyard.

With what just pride ladies have shown me some rose-bush, geranium, or calla lily, that they have nursed through the cold winter, till in early spring they were rewarded by a fragrant bloom of floral gratitude! How often I have gone with a happy amateur, to witness some unusual success achieved in his garden! If we were all amateurs in the vineyard of the Lord, throwing our hearts into the work of stimulating and training character into symmetrical, fruitful, deathless life, how this wilderness world would blossom! Too often we are like the hireling, whose aim seems merely to "put in the day" and get his "penny." But plants and human souls are alike in this, that they feel and recognize the touch of love; and the mystical and material garden both thrive doubly well under the care of those who work *con amore*, rather than officially.

But the saddest part of it all is, that the majority will not work at all in the way of producing anything of real value. They are like my cherry-tree, and all their native vigor and activity results in that which adds nothing to the well-being of the world.

What would I not give for the physical

strength and health of some of the young men above referred to, whose days are spent in smoking, reading questionable novels, dressing, dancing, flirting, driving, card-playing, etc.

With the exception of smoking (perhaps), the same occupations fill the days of multitudes of ladies. The result of their lives, put in a mathematical form, would be something as follows:

Mr. Augustus Le Grand = froth.

Miss Laura De Flirté = froth.

The world—both = to a garden with two weeds pulled out.

The parties themselves, if honest and *educated*, would admit this summing of their lives to be correct. It's rather strange that they are so contented, in view of the truth.

In the above light the cynical philosopher may justly regard those who, in a world so full of work, and in such need of work of all kinds, aim to be only idlers. On the Lycurgan principle of anything for the good of the state, they would be quietly strangled.

But the spirit of Christianity is opposite to all this, and leads us to look at this class as I did at my thrifty but worse than useless cherry-tree, whose fruit was only a large pit with a bitter skin drawn over it. If its abundant vitality, however, could be turned into useful channels —that is, into grafts of some excellent variety,— how much better thus to utilize life by conversion to noble ends, than to destroy it?

Early in April, therefore, every branch of sufficient size, from the top down, was grafted; and in due time they were nearly all growing finely, and I felt that I should now have a practical convert standing before my house, that would tend to inspire general confidence in my ministry.

But now comes in my irrational blunder, and one that I fear is too common on the part of reformers, as before stated. I had left a good many small branches scattered about the tree, but when the grafts commenced growing, I resolved that all the strength should go into them, that the old wild life should cease at once, and that I should have a cherry-tree saint from the start. Just as we often say to people that we are trying to lead to better things:

"You must do everything that is right, and nothing that is wrong."

So I said to my great rampant young tree, you must put all your power into those little scions five inches long, and develop those. All branches of your former doings must be stopped.

And what the result? Why, the shock was too great; the transition too sharp and short; and the tree, utterly discouraged seemingly, gave up in despair and died.

We read Paul's exhortation to "Grow in grace" as if it were "Jump into grace."

Nature, human and horticultural, improves by growth, and synods, councils, and reformers cannot change this Divine law. I am now satisfied that my wild young blade of a tree might have been converted into a most fruitful member of the garden; but it stood a long time a blasted monument of my blundering zeal, for I let it remain as a warning.

This subject of grafting, or horticultural conversion, is very suggestive, and has many analogies to moral experience. The earlier in life it takes place, the readier the growth and the better the chances, is a truism in both cases. Still, trees quite advanced in life can often be grafted to great advantage, and where space is limited, and trees of necessity must be few, quite a variety can soon be secured by putting in scions of different kinds. For instance, on the south side of an apple-tree, some good early or "harvest" variety might be grafted in the branches, a fall apple on the west side, and a late winter apple on the remaining boughs gradually, as we have shown, the whole strength of the tree could be thrown into these grafts, and the different kinds would grow amicably from one stem; indicating that a good man can be useful in more ways than one.

The same is true of a pear or a cherry tree; so that by judicious grafting we can bring all the fruit on our places up to a high standard.

Whenever we observe any unusually fine fruit, we can no doubt obtain permission from the possessor to cut a few scions. This should be done in March, before the buds swell; and the grafts should be kept in the cellar packed in moist sand or earth till we wish to use them, so that they may not shrivel. When the buds on the trees begin to show that the sap is flowing freely, then graft in the scions, and in a strong tree you probably have a little fruit in the third year.

But on one hand do not try to convert too fast by cutting back everything save the grafts; and on the other, convert as fast as you can safely, by gradually putting the whole strength of the tree into the grafts; for if but one branch of the old stock is left to have its own way for all time, it will crowd out and kill the approved varieties with certainty.

I am astonished that there is not a chair on grafting in our theological seminaries.

XVII.

CORN AND BEANS, ETC.—(SUCCOTASH.)

I LEAN to the Epicurean rather than to the Stoic philosophy. Indeed, as far as I am acquainted with the traditions of my childhood, I never was much of a Stoic in silent endurance of "outrageous fortune" armed (justly, I fear) with a rod, and I am satisfied that I was anything but nonchalant when her smiles meant mince-pie and jelly-cake. I suppose the man is wrapped up in the boy, just as the oak in the acorn. At any rate, I imagine that my heart will ever yearn over the place that ministers so much to every sense as the garden. Mine, as I have shown, furnishes me with music; and I have heard nothing at the academy in New York equal to the concerts given in the trees around our ivy-covered porch.

Why should I speak of the sense of sight! It seems like proving the self-evident and enlarging on an axiom. The genuine gardener enjoys seeing even a pumpkin grow, though the word " sprawl " is most characteristic of its existence. How great and varied are the pleasures that Nature provides when, in addition to being bountiful in exquisite flowers, she also gives to every fruit and vegetable some peculiar touch of grace and beauty.

Then there is the sense of smelling, which we do not half appreciate enough, perhaps because so often it is a misfortune. When we consider the millions who live in cities, and through whose open windows the zephyr blows direct from the gutter instead of a bed of mignonette, and the millions in the country who have a pig-sty near the house instead of a rose-arbor, it may be questioned whether the world would not be better off with four senses instead of five. It would seem, though, that to the latter class the choice of the two odors was a matter of taste, and that the near proximity of the sty and the absence of the roses indicated their preference.

But a man with a cultivated, indeed we may say broadly, a civilized nose, is blessed in a garden. We have all noticed how a drop or two of some powerful perfume falling on a book, table, or garment will distil its faint deliciousness for weeks and months. Not a little of the essence of Eden has fallen on the modern garden, and lingers there from early spring till winter. I do not refer to a cabbage patch on the wane, or anything else on the wane, which slovenly gardeners leave around; and it is not for me to irreverently dispute the voice of antiquity in regard to the onion. I must admire here as in some other cases that I cannot understand, the ancient wisdom of the world. Only great or rash souls willingly become heretics and trample on the authority of ages.

But my garden in the main is to my modern unsophisticated nose like the Spice Islands of the Pacific Ocean. Even the fresh-turned soil in spring, before a seed has germinated or a bud swollen, has a wholesome, grateful odor; and soon the reviving grass in the lawn, the opening of fragrant buds, and modest violets like timid blue eyes shyly watching you, the glowing crocus and wax-like hyacinths, and many others, all combine to fill Nature's censer that April winds swing to and fro. And if there is a piney grove near by, from which motherwort, anemones, and trailing arbutus can breathe their spirit into the floral service, with which the praise of the season opens, may I be there to worship also!

I have often asked myself, could anything in Paradise have surpassed some of our spring days, when the peach, plum, and cherry, and then the pear and apple trees, become huge bouquets? May and June are Nature's fairy festival—not the luxurious richness of midsummer, nor solid abundance of autumn, is then served up; but she spreads a dainty, delicate repast of dews and perfumes, of honey such as flowers distil, and all the glancing, airy creatures of the wing are invited. From every flowering tree comes the hum of small talk as innumerable honey-bees and yellow-jackets sip and gossip; while ever and anon some great humble-bee goes blundering and booming around, like some important and blustering master of ceremonies.

But the birds are the wassailers par excellence They eat and drink, sing, fight, and make love with an abandon that is quite human.

You need not tell me that they don't get "high," and that their extravagances may result only from their bird nature. I know very well that the bobolink who lived on the edge of my garden last summer was more than slightly inebriated several times when the apples were in blossom. In language more forcible than elegant, I maintain from what he said and did (the test we apply to our neighbors) that he was "tight," and if he was not, then I don't know the world and have never seen any one drink anything stronger than cambric tea. If he had belonged to any temperance organization he ought to have been disciplined. The truth was, he had been hanging around a large apple-tree in full bloom, all day, and when evening came, he could not sing straight, fly straight, or do anything decorously, but was the most jubilant, incoherent, rollicking little blade that ever went on a spree, and in the twilight tumbled into a clover-field to bed in a manner simply scandalous. Mr. Gough should turn his attention to the bobolinks.

What a chemist Nature is! How in the name of all that is wonderful can she manage to give every kind of flower and vegetable a different perfume? Some of the most homely and useful products of the garden give out odors that are as grateful as those of choice flowers, just as some human lives that are busiest and fullest of care have still the aroma of peace and rest about them.

"Well, well," growls some impatient reader, "what has the garden to do with the sense of touch?"

If you had blistered your hands with a hoe handle, I think you would know, my captious reader It will give you a man's hand instead of a woman's. (Now I have disgusted scores of the white-kid gentry.) I know modern society produces multitudes of women who like to be taken to the altar by men whose hands, incased in Jouvain's latest style, are almost as diminutive as their own. They may soon see the day, however, when they will wish that the man who offered his hand had offered little more in that line. But let her put him in the garden a while, and the lily fingers will soon grow more capable of wielding the weapons of life's battle.

But it was not with the Spartan idea of discipline and manly development that I first referred my garden as ministering to the sense of touch. It can do this as delicately and pleasurably as the viewless perfume. Pick off the opening leaves from a lilac bush, and their silken softness is as exquisite as their perfume. Varied foliage is as different to the sense of touch as to the eye. What sensation is more delicious than that of pressing your lips into the cool velvety centre of a double rose! It is the perfection of kissing, and without the slightest danger of scandal.

But after all our poetry and sentiment, it is when we come to the sense of taste, what we put in our mouths, that we realize what the garden does for us. The most practical souls can appreciate this phase of the subject. All want what comes from the garden, and so the gardener thrives. He need never starve whose business is to supply a universal need, nor does a man work with less unction when, in helping to supply the world in general, he is also supplying himself in particular. Basing my belief on the sense of taste, I know that the reader will enter into my feelings as I set about the labors of later spring, the time when we prepare to secure some of the chief delicacies of the garden.

We will suppose that all the fruits of the garden and orchard are properly set out and cared for, as they ought to be by this time, and will turn our attention to those annual vegetables not yet specially mentioned, that mature in the summer and fall.

I have found early beets a profitable crop in my locality, and in '71 sold three hundred and eight bunches for thirty dollars and twenty-two cents. Having tried several varieties, I prefer the "Extra Early Bassano" for market purpose. The "Egyptian Blood" is an excellent variety, did its name not make one's flesh creep, and cause you to feel something like a cannibal. The Bassano variety may be sown even till the end of July, and will make good roots by October, but the best crops are secured from early sowings. I prefer to plant as early in April as the ground is dry enough. By putting the seed at this time in a warm light soil, and covering it with old black rotted manure, a very early crop can be secured.

Any one following this course will be in advance of his neighbors, and will obtain excellent prices. I have often sown radishes with my beets, but have come to the conclusion, that it does not pay, since the former retard the latter to such a degree that no gain is secured. Frequent stirring of the ground around the young plants greatly stimulates their growth. When they are about four inches high, thin them out, so that they will stand three or four inches from each other in the row, and let the rows be one foot apart. These thinnings make excellent spinach, and many will buy them for that purpose. So do not be too economical of seed, as it is far better to thin out, than plant over. When it is desired to raise the largest and latest crop, the soil should be cooler and moister in its nature, and in every case should be very rich.

Cabbages and cauliflowers wintered over in cold frames should, of course, be set out in the open ground as soon as it can be nicely worked, and by the first of May they should be growing finely. But those grown under glass from seed sown in the spring, should not be put out till the weather is quite warm and settled, and all danger of severe frost is over. Though naturally hardy plants, they are not so when forced in hot-beds or even cold frames. After being placed in the open ground, nothing does more good than frequent stirrings of the soil around them. Be careful also never to set them, if it can be helped, where any of the cabbage family, or even turnips or radishes, have been grown the year before; for if you do, you will very likely lose your crop with that pest of the garden, the "club-foot," which renders the root a diseased solid mass. This evil is so great in my grounds, that I have almost given up contending with it; and in '71 my sales of cabbage and cauliflowers unitedly only amounted to seven dollars and eighty-nine cents. But where one has plenty of good strong land, and can put the cabbage on new ground every year, he will find it one of the most profitable of crops. The tastes of fallen man lean toward cabbage almost as universally as toward the onion, and there is a large demand for it in every market.

Carrots, though more truly a farm crop, deserve a place in the garden. The Long Orange is the best variety. I give a little space to it every year, and find that it pays well. During the summer there is a demand for carrots bunched like beets or radishes, and to meet this it is perhaps best to plant the Early Horn variety. The seed of the last-named kind should be sown as soon as the frost is out. But even for early use I would rather employ the Long Orange, and if planted as soon as possible in spring, it will meet the summer demand in a local market, and what remain make large fine roots for winter. A good deal of latitude in time is allowed in sowing this seed, and the farmers (who are enterprising enough to raise them) put in their main crop in June. Any one in the country keeping a cow or even a horse ought to raise a large quantity, as they would in this way cheaply provide one of the best kinds of feed, and one that would make all other kinds of fodder more beneficial. Even if there were but a limited market for this vegetable it would pay to raise it, for a comparatively small piece of ground will yield so largely as to reduce the expenses of keeping a cow and horse nearly one half.

Celery seed should be sown as soon in April as the ground becomes light and warm. Make the rows seven or eight inches apart, and cover the seed very lightly. The only further care required till July is to keep the ground clear of weeds, and not to let the plants grow too thickly, and therefore weak and spindling. Thin out, and the last of June mow off the tops of the young plants in the seed-bed. This makes them strong and stocky, and much more apt to live when set out in the trenches or open ground.

About the last of April or first of May, seed for late or winter cabbage should be sown, remembering the precautions that we have before urged. About the last of June the young plants will be large enough for transferral to the place where they are to head.

A little lettuce seed of the Neapolitan, Malta, or large Indian varieties may be sown also for the summer supply. These kinds make very large heads, and are best adapted for hot weather. Then set out in rich soil; the plants standing fifteen inches apart. After the first of

June there is no call for lettuce worth mentioning in my market.

I rarely sow spinach in the spring, expecting a full supply from that started in the fall. In many localities, it might pay well to raise a summer crop of this. The gardener who has strong, heavy land, in which this vegetable would not winter over well, might find it very profitable to sow the seed in the spring. He certainly would, if he could find a good market in June, and then he would have his ground clear for celery or some late crop.

Early turnips have never payed in my garden, though I have tried them several times. Experience in other localities might reverse this. The seed should be sown as soon as the frost is out, and sown thickly, for the black fly will want his share. Thin out, so that the roots will be at least six inches apart in the row. Lime dusted over the young plants is said to keep off the insects, but I find nothing like little chickens.

For the last two or three years, I have only raised a few very early potatoes for home use. They are a farm crop, and as I can raise a bushel of strawberries almost as easily as the potatoes, I prefer to take the nine dollars that the latter will bring, and buy nine bushels of potatoes. And yet, if one had plenty of land adapted to the growth of this " corner-stone " vegetable, and kept a horse, so that nearly all the work could be done with a plough, it would no doubt pay well to raise the Early Rose. I have known them to sell as high as three dollars a bushel, and a good crop at one dollar and fifty cents would be very satisfactory. If it is possible that I have a reader who does not know how to cultivate the potato, let him ask the first Irishman he meets, and he will get an answer not far out of the way. At the same time, there is scarcely a vegetable, with which soil, locality, and culture make a greater difference; and those raised on a sandy loam are often as much better than those from wet land, as light bread than dough.

I have always found, that a small space devoted to cucumbers paid well, and of course the home market must be supplied with this vegetable. A crisp young cucumber, picked with the dew on it, and sliced for breakfast, is as different from the wilted article often found in city markets, as sweet sixteen from sixty.

As I have said before, it is best to make the hills quite early in the season. This can be done by opening small round holes, four feet apart each way, and filling them with mingled soil and old rotted manure, heaping all up into little mounds for the sun to warm and mellow. Then, some time from the first to the tenth of May, these can be levelled down and the seed planted. It is best to plant from fifteen to twenty seeds in each hill, so that the bugs may have their share and still leave some for the grower. They are not at all considerate, but take all they can, and my plan is to have more than they can destroy; just as your cool generals calculate they can carry a point, and still lose three-fourths of the men they start with. At the same time, like the generals, you must kill all the opposing bugs you can.

Musk and water melons require similar treatment. If the ground is light and inclined to drouth, the hills should be made level with ground around; but if heavy and damp, a rise of six inches would be of benefit.

I also make cold frames very useful in growing cucumbers. About the first of May, the lettuce and radish crops in them are all sold, and the large English varieties of " cucs,' as the truckmen call them, or if preferred, the good old standard kind, the "Improved White Spined," can be planted and covered with glass. With this artificial heat they will come forward very rapidly, and if kept well aired and watered, will give a fine and early yield. Some hasten the crop very much, by placing a small box covered with four panes of glass over the hills in the open garden. Plants so protected can be started by the middle of April.

The curious reader has doubtless failed to see, thus far, the bearing of these pages on the suggestive Indian word "Succotash," with which I commenced this chapter. This has been on the good old principle, that we try to save the best till the last. It is probably known, that this savory dish which crowns our dinner tables in July and August, is a relic of the red-man; and it is the one Indian antiquity that I am specially interested in. The vanished tribes will never be forgotten while corn and beans grow, and this happy combination, which they taught to the pale face, quite comforts us for their absence. Succotash may not be quite so romantic as war-whoops and scalpings, but then we belong to a practical age.

But before we revel in this heathen dainty, we must, like the mythical Hiawatha, wrestle with Mondamin, "conquer and overcome" him,

> "Make a bed for him to lie in
> Where the rain may fall upon him,
> Where the sun may come and warm him."

In other words, we must first plant our corn.

Happily, the raising of this delicious vegetable is no great mystery. The Indian squaws succeeded well with it, and in view of this fact no manly and civilized gardener would like to admit of failure. A rich light soil and good culture rarely fail in giving a good crop year after year. There is almost a universal demand for it in every market, and by planting the different kinds, and by successive plantings from the first of May till the last of June, a good supply can be maintained a long time. A little well-rotted manure in the hill with the seed greatly hastens and strengthens its growth. I have found the "Early Crosby, Early Eight Rowed, and Stowell's Late Evergreen," the best varieties.

Where the corn is grown some distance from the house, the crows are often troublesome. They are said to be a very sagacious bird, and having once found a row, will go up and down it, seemingly knowing just where to look for the hills. My father once had an old colored gardener, who made the rows so crooked that the crows could not find them, for having never been to Congress they expected things to be on the square.

I also recall a story that I have heard which suggests another remedy. I can vouch for the fact that this story has really been told, and by an ancient man, not woman, and this is more than can be said of many stories. If the result was more favorable to crow nature than to human nature, that is a fault of the facts.

Once upon a time a man planted corn, and the crows dug it up. The aforesaid man had great faith in whiskey; but the aforesaid crows knew nothing about whiskey. The man thought that if he soaked some corn in the "fusel," and put it in the field, the crows might become so thoroughly corned that he could catch, preserve, and hang them up as warnings, so that their companions might shun the place where there was danger of getting into a like pickle. The experiment turned out differently, but even better than he expected. For a crow soon appeared and gorged himself with the spirit-soaked corn. The consequences were quite human. From his crop it went to his head, which soon felt "queer," then dizzy. He tried to step off in his wonted stately manner, but tumbled into a furrow. He staggered up a corn-hill, and stood there, in bewildered, helpless imbecility, blinking at the trees and fences that seemed dancing a hornpipe in the spring sunshine.

Just at this inopportune moment a dozen or more crows came sailing toward the field, bent on a good square meal from their accustomed "pickings and stealings," as a politician would express himself, when something in the peculiar appearance of their "discouraged" companion arrested their attention, and they gathered round him with no slight *caws* for wonder. The sanguine man that had soaked the corn, that had "corned" the crow, expected to see all the rest follow suit, like so many of his neighbors. He hardly expected to find a higher standard of virtue in his corn-field than in that social centre, the village tavern. But for once, at least, it was proved that there is honor among thieves, for the robbers stood around their staggering fellow, grave and remonstrative, and seemingly much scandalized. Then from being stupidly drunk, the crow became pugnaciously drunk, and wanted to fight them all around for nothing, *à la* "Sixth Ward." From this he passed on to the maudlin and sentimental stage, and offered some uncouth gallantries to the oldest and most sedate crow of the party.

This was past endurance. There was a brief clamorous council, and with an expression of unmingled disgust resting on their usually solemn and sanctimonious faces, they took wing and were seen no more.

"Consider the ravens," O ye children of men! It only remains to be said that the inebriated crow thus socially "cut' and ostracized, not having a gutter to lie in, like lordly man, did the next best thing possible, and tumbled head first into a furrow; from whence the man, the Mephistopheles of the plot, took him, and hung him up in black, as warning to other crows—would that I could add, to other men.

Happy termination. The corn grew and prospered, and became the first ingredient of the delicious Indian compound.

There is no occasion to enlarge greatly on beans. People of average intelligence are expected to know this vegetable.

The two varieties that I have found most profitable are the "Dwarf German Wax," as a bush bean, and the "Large Lima," for poles. Of the former twenty-three and one-fourth bushels were sold for fifty-one dollars; of the latter, nineteen and one-eighth bushels, for thirty-six dollars and seventy-seven cents.

The Dwarf German Wax can be planted very early, and they seem quite hardy. I have succeeded well with those put in light warm ground, quite early in April. This variety needs rich soil, and rotted manure drilled in with the seed is of great advantage. The limas should not be planted till about the tenth of May in our latitude, as they cannot endure cold or wet weather. Unless the ground of the garden is rich and light, it is well to prepare the hills around poles, as described for cucumbers.

Many lose their first plantings by covering too deeply. Limas should be pushed under the soil about an inch only, eye or germ downwards. Seemingly they do not like being buried, and soon reappear again, thus tending to substantiate the ghost theory still so prevalent. Not unfrequently the surprised amateur has poked them back again and then they stayed, but the poles remained bare. If you want to obtain anything from Nature, treat her as "lovely woman," and let her have her own way as far as possible, however odd her methods.

Arbitrary measures won't answer, as some of my readers outside of the garden may have discovered.

I now consider that I have done all in my power to secure succotash, and therefore happiness, to my readers. May not come grateful sighs of memory mingled with the mouthsful next July? If what is esteemed the profoundest human philosophy be true, I have gained some hold on the popular heart.

We close with a few marriages, as all orthodox stories should.

It now but remains to link the labors of late spring and of summer with those before described, as appropriately commencing with autumn, and then to bow myself out.

The tomato has probably been the most profitable vegetable that I have raised. It will grow on any soil, and after being once started, requires but little attention. The main point is to have good, strong, stocky plants by the 10th of May, to set out in the open ground. Everyone can grow tomatoes, and nearly every one does, who has a few feet of land ; and since they will flourish where a weed will live, success crowns the most careless culture. But in having tomatoes very early, any amount of skill and effort can be expended. In the height of the season, there are times when they will not sell at any price, while I have sold those first ripening at twelve cents a quart. Therefore every year we have half a dozen or more " novelties " introduced, each said to be earlier than anything ever grown before. But gardeners are annually losing their childlike faith in regard to these. Still try a few. It is an innocent form of gambling and will add interest to the garden. But we would advise that the main supply be of the "Solid Smooth Red," "Trophy," and "General Grant." I am going to try the "General" four years longer. But in order to be first in the market, sow the seed of some very early variety in a hot-bed as soon in March as you can, and about the middle of April transfer the plants to a deep cold frame, where the glass will be at least two feet from the bottom of the pit. Set them out six or eight inches apart, so that the plants will grow bushy and strong. Give plenty of air in the heat of the day, and in *warm* rains take off the glass altogether. Thus the plants will be very vigorous and hardy by May 10th. Set them out in a warm and rather dry spot in the open garden, and do not let the soil be too rich, as this tends to growth of vines rather than fruit, and you will beat your neighbors, which is a very proper thing for a gardener to do. My sales in '71 were eighty-two and one-fourth bushels, realizing one hundred and twenty-five dollars and sixty cents. In '72 the results were not very different. A great many pretty experiments can be tried in pruning and training the tomato, which the amateur's genius or leisure will suggest. The majority of us are satisfied to set out the plants and hoe them.

We next come to the treatment of the strawberry-beds previous to their fruiting, and can assure the reader that the crop can be greatly enhanced by proper culture, during April and especially May. In the first place, if it was not done in fall, a good top-dressing of manure in the early spring stimulates the plants very much. If the manure is fine, it can be scattered immediately over the plants, as well as around them. If they were covered with coarse manure in the fall, then this can be forked in between the rows in April. Good cultivation, frequent stirrings of the soil until they begin to blossom, adds to their vigor greatly; but as soon as the fruit commences to form, the roots should be in no way disturbed, but another and entirely different course adopted, which, probably carried out, often works wonders. I refer to judicious mulching.

Say that the soil between the rows is light, and free of weeds, as it ought to be. Then after the first rain, when the ground has been well moistened, cover the intervening spaces between the plants thickly and closely with leaves, or better still, fresh grass just cut from the lawn. Only unparalleled drouth will greatly injure the bed so treated. The berries will be much larger and finer, and the plants continue longer in bearing. Moreover, the fruit will be perfectly clean, and will need no washing for the table; a process that robs it of flavor and beauty. For these reasons, it is far better to keep the plants in straight rows, as the ground can then be readily covered with grass, leaves, or straw, at the time of blossoming. Where the beds have been permitted to run together, or where they are cultivated in wide, matted rows, it is next to impossible to mulch them well, and they are very apt to suffer from drouth This was the case with my beds in '71. I could not bring myself to cut out the strong, thrifty plants, so as to leave good spaces between the rows. The ground was rich, so I concluded to let all fruit. If May had been cool and moist (the weather that the strawberry delights in), my crop would have been enormous. But, from the middle of May till some time in June, we had a very unusual drouth. I tried watering, as before intimated, and perhaps helped some of my beds very much, but others, I think, were injured. It is well known to gardeners that if you once commence watering in a dry time, you must continue, or the plants will suffer far more than if left to fight it out themselves. If you can thoroughly soak your beds and keep them moist, watering always in the evening, they will do splendidly. But if you water in the morning, or while the sun shines, the plants will be scalded and the fruit injured; and if the ground is left to dry out thoroughly after an artificial watering, still greater harm will be done. My difficulties and losses in trying to water a large area are thus plainly indicated, even though I had the water drawn in a barrel by a horse. Still, as I have stated, I raised fifty-seven bushels of fruit on five-eighths of an acre, but am satisfied that the same number of plants, kept in rows and mulched, would have yielded over seventy bushels, and at less cost and culture.

On the 31st of May three quarts were picked What though they were sour, as the first ripening always are? They were big and red, with something of the ambrosial strawberry flavor, and had the exquisite aroma that almost rivals the rose.

As has been hinted, it is the time-honored custom of story-tellers to marry off some of their principal characters in their closing chapter. I have already united my corn and beans in the delightful combination of succotash. Single beans and single corn are very well, but they are much better together. Good marriages always improve character.

It still remains for me to provide for my blushing strawberries and delicate raspberries, and for them "nobody and nothing" is good enough, but cream from our Alderney cow. The happy fruit is picked for breakfast with the dew upon it for wedding diamonds.

> And when the cream appears,
> Is soon "o'er head and ears."

Who would not be a gardener, when **he**

could solemnize such unions three times a day? Do not imagine that you can do this as well in the city as the country. There may be more parade of silver and gold in the service, but city berries are too often like city belles; city cream like Wall Street men. They have seen too much of the world.

To change a subject that may not be agreeable to all, we turn to one somewhat in contrast, and remark that winter cabbage should be set out before the Fourth of July, in our latitude, and it would be better that the large late varieties were growing in the open ground the last of June.

I might refer to other vegetables, from which some slight revenue was obtained, or might be; but as this is mainly a record of experience, they scarcely have place in these pages. If this treatise is in any sense exhaustive, it deserves such character solely from its effect on the reader.

We will, therefore, close with celery, the latest, and perhaps the most delicious vegetable of the garden.

Before the 10th of August, it should all be in the trenches, where it is to grow and blanch. Some prefer to set out the plants on level ground, in rows four or five feet apart, and doubtless this is the most economical way of raising it by the quantity, especially where the dwarf varieties are used. I have practised both methods with success. A very rich soil is indispensable for this crop. In fall it is my plan to draw the earth up around the plants about once a week, so that the blanching process will go forward with the growth.

I much prefer storing my celery in the open garden during the winter. It is very easily and simply done. Selecting some gravelly slope where there is thorough drainage, I have a trench cut, a foot wide and about the depth of the celery's length, so that when packed close in the trench, in the natural position in which it grew, its top leaves will be a little above the surface of the ground. As the weather grows colder, late in November, the earth can be drawn up till the leaves are nearly all covered. This should not be done till freezing weather has really come, for too early and close earthing up might cause decay. Just before winter sets in, cover heavily with leaves or straw. Thus all frost will be kept out, and you will be able to get at the plants any time. Under this treatment they will usually keep in excellent order till spring.

I prefer to get my celery plants nicely growing during July. Places from which early crops were taken furnish the needed space, and this is put in readiness by the most thorough enriching of the soil. As my ground is limited, and as I raise the large varieties, I usually prepare trenches about eight inches deep and eighteen wide for the plants. Then we are on the watch for showers, so as to get as many out as possible before the rain.

Sometimes we have three or four showers a day, and the cloud scenery resulting is often marvellously beautiful; but usually they make their appearance some hot afternoon about three or four o'clock.

A person living in the city can have little idea of thunder-storms as they occur in this mountain region. The hills about us, while they attract the electrified clouds, are also our protection, for, abounding in iron ore, they become huge lightning-rods above the houses and hamlets at their bases. But little recks old Bear Mountain, or Cro' Nest, Jove's most fiery bolts. The rocky splinters fly for a moment; some oak or chestnut comes quivering down; but soon the mosses, like kindly charity, have covered up the wounded rock, and three or four saplings have grown from the roots of the blighted tree.

But the storm we witness from our safe and sheltered homes is often grand beyond description. At first, in the distant west, a cloud rises so dark that you can scarcely distinguish it from a blue highland. But a low muttering of thunder vibrates through the sultry air, and we know what is coming. Soon the afternoon sun is shaded, and a deep, unnatural twilight settles upon the landscape, like the shadow of a great sorrow on a face that was smiling a moment before. The thunder grows heavier, like the rumble and roar of an approaching battle. The western arch of the sky is black as night. The eastern arch is bright and sunny, and as you glance from side to side, you cannot but think of those who, comparatively innocent and happy at first, cloud their lives in maturer years with evil and crime, and darken the future with the wrath of heaven. At last the vanguard of black flying clouds, disjointed, jagged, the rough skirmish line of the advancing storm, is over our heads. Back of these, in one dark, solid mass, comes the tempest. For a moment there is a sort of hush of expectation, like the lull before a battle. The trees on the distant brow of a mountain are seen to toss and writhe, but as yet no sound is heard. Soon there is a faint, far-away rushing noise, the low, deep prelude of Nature's grand musical discord that is to follow. There is a vivid flash, and a startling peal of thunder breaks forth overhead, and rolls away with countless reverberations among the hills. In the meantime the distant rushing sound has developed into an increasing roar. Half way down the mountain side the trees are swaying wildly. At the base stands a grove, motionless, expectant, like a square of infantry awaiting an impetuous cavalry charge. In a moment it comes. At first the shock seems terrible. Every branch bends low. Dead limbs rattle down like hail. Leaves torn away fly wildly through the air. But the sturdy trunks stand their ground, and the baffled tempest passes on. Mingling with the rush of the wind and reverberations of thunder, a new sound, a new part now enters into the grand harmony. At first it is a low, continuous roar, caused by the falling rain upon the leaves. It grows louder fast, like the pattering feet of a coming multitude. Then the great drops fall around, yards apart, like scattering shots. They grow closer, and soon a streaming torrent drives you to shelter. The next heavy peal is to the eastward, showing that the bulk of the shower is past. The roar of the thunder dies away down the river. The thickly falling rain contracts your vision to a narrow circle, out of which Cozzens's great hotel and Bear Mountain loom vaguely. The flowers and shrubbery bend to the moisture with the air of one who stands and takes it. The steady, continuous plash upon the roof slackens into a quiet pattering of rain-drops. The west is lightening up; by and by a long line of blue is seen above Cro' Nest. The setting sun shines out upon a purified and more beautiful landscape. Every leaf, every spire of grass is brilliant with gems of moisture. The cloud scenery has all changed. The sun is setting in unclouded splendor. Not the west but the east is now black with storm; but the rainbow, emblem of hope and God's mercy, spans its blackness, and in the skies we again have suggested to us a life, once clouded and darkly threatened by evil, but now, through penitence and reform, ending in peace and beauty, God spanning the wrong of the past with His rich and varied promises of forgiveness. At last the skies are clear again. Along the eastern horizon the retreating storm sends up occasional flashes, that seem like regretful thoughts of the past. Then night comes on, cool, moonlit, breathless. Not a leaf stirs where an hour before the sturdiest limbs bent to the earth. This must be Nature's commentary on the "peace that passeth all understanding."

SENT FREE ON APPLICATION.

DESCRIPTIVE CATALOGUE

—OF—

RURAL BOOKS,

CONTAINING 116 8vo. PAGES,

PROFUSELY ILLUSTRATED, AND GIVING FULL DESCRIPTIONS OF NEARLY 600 WORKS ON THE FOLLOWING SUBJECTS:

Farm and Garden,
   Fruits, Flowers, Etc.
      Cattle, Sheep, and Swine,
 Dogs, Horses, Riding, Etc.,
    Poultry, Pigeons, and Bees,
       Angling and Fishing,
Boating, Canoeing, and Sailing,
   Field Sports and Natural History,
      Hunting, Shooting, Etc.,
 Architecture and Building,
    Landscape Gardening,
      Household and Miscellaneous

PUBLISHERS AND IMPORTERS:

ORANGE JUDD COMPANY,

52 & 54 Lafayette Place, New York.

Books will be Forwarded, postpaid, on receipt of Price.

Mushrooms: How to Grow Them.

Any one who has an ordinary house cellar, woodshed or barn, can grow Mushrooms. This is the most practical work on the subject ever written, and the only book on growing Mushrooms published in America. The author describes how he grows Mushrooms, and how they are grown for profit by the leading market gardeners, and for home use by the most successful private growers. Engravings drawn from nature expressly for this work. By Wm. Falconer. Cloth. Price, postpaid. 1.50

Land Draining.

A Handbook for Farmers on the Principles and Practice of Draining, by Manly Miles, giving the results of his extended experience in laying tile drains. The directions for the laying out and the construction of tile drains will enable the farmer to avoid the errors of imperfect construction, and the disappointment that must necessarily follow. This manual for practical farmers will also be found convenient for references in regard to many questions that may arise in crop growing, aside from the special subjects of drainage of which it treats. Cloth, 12mo. 1.00

Allen's New American Farm Book.

The very best work on the subject; comprising all that can be condensed into an available volume. Originally by Richard L. Allen. Revised and greatly enlarged by Lewis F. Allen. Cloth, 12mo. 2.50

Henderson's Gardening for Profit.

By Peter Henderson. The standard work on Market and Family Gardening. The successful experience of the author for more than thirty years, and his willingness to tell, as he does in this work, the secret of his success for the benefit of others, enables him to give most valuable information. The book is profusely illustrated. Cloth, 12mo. 2.00

Henderson's Gardening for Pleasure.

A guide to the amateur in the fruit, vegetable and flower garden, with full descriptions for the greenhouse, conservatory and window garden. It meets the wants of all classes in country, city and village who keep a garden for their own enjoyment rather than for the sale of products. By Peter Henderson. Finely Illustrated. Cloth, 12mo. 2.00

Johnson's How Crops Grow.

New Edition. A Treatise on the Chemical Composition, Structure and Life of the Plant. Revised Edition. This book is a guide to the knowledge of agricultural plants, their composition, their structure and modes of development and growth; of the complex organizations of plants, and the use of the parts; the germination of seeds, and the food of plants obtained both from the air and the soil. The book is a valuable one to all real students of agriculture. With numerous illustrations and tables of analysis. By Prof. Samuel W. Johnson of Yale College. Cloth. 12mo 2.00

STANDARD BOOKS.

Johnson's How Crops Feed.

A Treatise on the Atmosphere and the Soil, as related in the Nutrition of Agricultural Plants. This volume—the companion and complement to "How Crops Grow"—has been welcomed by those who appreciate the scientific aspects of agriculture. Illustrated. By Prof. Samuel W. Johnson. Cloth, 12mo. 2.00

Market Gardening and Farm Notes.

By Barnet Landreth. Experiences and Observations for both North and South, of interest to the Amateur Gardener, Trucker and Farmer. A novel feature of the book is the calendar of farm and garden operations for each month of the year; the chapters on fertilizers, transplanting, succession and rotation of crops, the packing, shipping and marketing of vegetables, will be especially useful to market gardeners. Cloth, 12mo. 1.00

Forest Planting.

A Treatise on the Care of Woodlands and the Restoration of the Denuded Timber-Lands on Plains and Mountains. By H. Nicholas Jarchow, LL. D. The author has fully described those European methods which have proved to be most useful in maintaining the superb forests of the old world. This experience has been adapted to the different climates and trees of America, full instructions being given for forest planting on our various kinds of soil and subsoil, whether on mountain or valley. Illustrated, 12mo. 1.50

Harris' Talks on Manures.

By Joseph Harris, M. S., author of "Walks and Talks on the Farm," "Harris on the Pig," etc. Revised and enlarged by the author. A series of familiar and practical talks between the author and the Deacon, the Doctor, and other neighbors, on the whole subject of manures and fertilizers; including a chapter especially written for it, by Sir John Bennet Lawes of Rothamsted, England. Cloth, 12mo. 1.75

Truck Farming at the South.

A work which gives the experience of a successful grower of vegetables or "truck" for Northern markets. Essential to any one who contemplates entering this promising field of Agriculture. By A. Oemler of Georgia. Illustrated, cloth, 12mo. 1.50

Sweet Potato Culture.

Giving full instructions from starting the plants to harvesting and storing the crop. With a chapter on the Chinese Yam. By James Fitz, Keswich, Va., author of "Southern Apple and Peach Culture." Cloth, 12mo. .60

Heinrich's Window Flower Garden.

The author is a practical florist, and this enterprising volume embodies his personal experiences in Window Gardening during a long period. New and enlarged edition. By Julius J. Heinrich. Fully illustrated. Cloth, 12mo. .75

Greenhouse Construction.

By Prof. L. R. Taft. A complete treatise on Greenhouse structures and arrangements of the various forms and styles of Plant Houses for professional florists as well as amateurs. All the best and most approved structures are so fully and clearly described that anyone who desires to build a Greenhouse will have no difficulty in determining the kind best suited to his purpose. The modern and most successful methods of heating and ventilating are fully treated upon. Special chapters are devoted to houses used for the growing of one kind of plants exclusively. The construction of hotbeds and frames receives appropriate attention. Over one hundred excellent illustrations, specially engraved for this work, make every point clear to the reader and add considerably to the artistic appearance of the book. Cloth, 12mo. 1.50

Bulbs and Tuberous-Rooted Plants.

By C. L. Allen. A complete treatise on the History, Description, Methods of Propagation and full Directions for the successful culture of Bulbs in the garden, Dwelling and Greenhouse. As generally treated, bulbs are an expensive luxury, while, when properly managed, they afford the greatest amount of pleasure at the least cost. The author of this book has for many years made bulb growing a specialty, and is a recognized authority on their cultivation and management. The illustrations which embellish this work have been drawn from nature, and have been engraved especially for this book. The cultural directions are plainly stated, practical and to the point. Cloth, 12mo. 2.00

Henderson's Practical Floriculture.

By Peter Henderson. A guide to the successful propagation and cultivation of florists' plants. The work is not one for florists and gardeners only, but the amateur's wants are constantly kept in mind, and we have a very complete treatise on the cultivation of flowers under glass, or in the open air, suited to those who grow flowers for pleasure as well as those who make them a matter of trade. Beautifully illustrated. New and enlarged edition. Cloth, 12mo. 1.50

Long's Ornamental Gardening for Americans.

A Treatise on Beautifying Homes, Rural Districts and Cemeteries. A plain and practical work at a moderate price, with numerous illustrations and instructions so plain that they may be readily followed. By Elias A. Long, Landscape Architect. Illustrated, Cloth, 12mo. 2.00

The Propagation of Plants.

By Andrew S. Fuller. Illustrated with numerous engravings. An eminently practical and useful work. Describing the process of hybridizing and crossing species and varieties, and also the many different modes by which cultivated plants may be propagated and multiplied. Cloth. 12mo. 1.50

STANDARD BOOKS.

Parsons on the Rose.

By Samuel B. Parsons. A treatise on the propagation, culture and history of the rose. New and revised edition. In his work upon the rose, Mr. Parsons has gathered up the curious legends concerning the flower, and gives us an idea of the esteem in which it was held in former times. A simple garden classification has been adopted, and the leading varieties under each class enumerated and briefly described. The chapters on multiplication, cultivation and training are very full, and the work is altogether one of the most complete before the public. Illustrated. Cloth, 12mo. 1.00

Henderson's Handbook of Plants.

This new edition comprises about fifty per cent. more genera than the former one, and embraces the botanical name, derivation, natural order, etc., together with a short history of the different genera, concise instructions for their propagation and culture, and all the leading local or common English names, together with a comprehensive glossary of Botanical and Technical terms. Plain instructions are also given for the cultivation of the principal vegetables, fruits and flowers. Cloth, large 8vo. 4.00

Barry's Fruit Garden.

By P. Barry. A standard work on Fruit and Fruit Trees; the author having had over thirty years' practical experience at the head of one of the largest nurseries in this country. New edition revised up to date. Invaluable to all fruit growers. Illustrated. Cloth, 12mo. 2.00

Fulton's Peach Culture.

This is the only practical guide to Peach Culture on the Delaware Peninsula, and is the best work upon the subject of peach growing for those who would be successful in that culture in any part of the country. It has been thoroughly revised and a large portion of it rewritten, by Hon. J. Alexander Fulton, the author, bringing it down to date. Cloth, 12mo. 1.50

Strawberry Culturist.

By Andrew S. Fuller. Containing the History, Sexuality, Field and Garden Culture of Strawberries, forcing or pot culture, how to grow from seed, hybridizing, and all information necessary to enable everybody to raise their own strawberries, together with a description of new varieties and a list of the best of the old sorts. Fully illustrated. Flexible cloth, 12mo. .25

Fuller's Small Fruit Culturist.

By Andrew S. Fuller. Rewritten, enlarged, and brought fully up to the present time. The book covers the whole ground of propagating Small Fruits, their culture, varieties, packing for market, etc. It is very finely and thoroughly illustrated, and makes an admirable companion to "The Grape Culturist," by the same well known author. 1.50

STANDARD BOOKS.

Fuller's Grape Culturist.
By A. S. Fuller. This is one of the very best or works on the Culture of the Hardy Grapes, with full directions for all departments of propagation, culture, etc., with 150 excellent engravings, illustrating planting, training, grafting, etc. Cloth, 12mo. 1.50

Quinn's Pear Culture for Profit.
Teaching How to Raise Pears Intelligently, and with the best results, how to find out the character of the soil, the best methods of preparing it, the best varieties to select under existing conditions, the best modes of planting, pruning, fertilizing, grafting, and utilizing the ground before the trees come into bearing, and finally of gathering and packing for market. Illustrated. By P. T. Quinn, practical horticulturist. Cloth, 12mo. 1.00

Husmann's American Grape Growing and Wine-Making.
By George Husmann of Talcoa vineyards, Napa, California. New and enlarged edition. With contributions from well know grape-growers, giving a wide range of experience. The author of this book is a recognized authority on the subject. Cloth, 12mo. 1.50

White's Cranberry Culture.
Contents:—Natural History.—History of Cultivation.—Choice of Location.—Preparing the Ground.—Planting the Vines.—Management of Meadows.—Flooding.—Enemies and Difficulties Overcome.—Picking.—Keeping.—Profit and Loss.—Letters from Practical Growers.—Insects Injurious to the Cranberry. By Joseph J. White, a practical grower. Illustrated. Cloth, 12mo. New and revised edition. 1.25

Fuller's Practical Forestry.
A Treatise on the Propagation, Planting and Cultivation, with a description and the botanical and proper names of all the indigenous trees of the United States, both Evergreen and Deciduous, with Notes on a large number of the most valuable Exotic Species. By Andrew S. Fuller, author of "Grape Culturist," "Small Fruit Culturist," etc. 1.50

Stewart's Irrigation for the Farm, Garden and Orchard.
This work is offered to those American Farmers and other cultivators of the soil who, from painful experience, can readily appreciate the losses which result from the scarcity of water at critical periods. By Henry Stewart. Fully illustrated. Cloth, 12mo. 1.50

Quinn's Money in the Garden.
By P. T. Quinn. The author gives in a plain, practical style, instructions on three distinct, although closely connected branches of gardening—the kitchen garden, market garden, and field culture, from successful practical experience for a term of years. Illustrated. Cloth, 12mo. 1.50

STANDARD BOOKS.

Roe's Play and Profit in My Garden.

By E. P. Roe. The author takes us to his garden on the rocky hillsides in the vicinity of West Point, and shows us how out of it, after four years' experience, he evoked a profit of $1,000, and this while carrying on pastoral and literary labor. It is very rarely that so much literary taste and skill are mated to so much agricultural experience and good sense. Cloth, 12mo. 1.50

The New Onion Culture.

By T. Greiner. This new work is written by one of our most successful agriculturists, and is full of new, original, and highly valuable matter of material interest to every one who raises onions in the family garden, or by the acre for market. By the process here described a crop of 2000 bushels per acre can be as easily raised as 500 or 600 bushels in the old way. Paper, 12mo. .50

The Dairyman's Manual.

By Henry Stewart, author of "The Shepherd's Manual," "Irrigation," etc. A useful and practical work, by a writer who is well known as thoroughly familiar with the subject of which he writes. Cloth, 12mo. 2.00

Allen's American Cattle.

Their History, Breeding and Management. By Lewis F. Allen. This book will be considered indispensable by every breeder of live stock. The large experience of the author in improving the character of American herds adds to the weight of his observations and has enabled him to produce a work which will at once make good his claims as a standard authority on the subject. New and revised edition. Illustrated. Cloth, 12mo. 2.50

Profits in Poultry.

Useful and ornamental Breeds and their Profitable Management. This excellent work contains the combined experience of a number of practical men in all departments of poultry raising. It is profusely illustrated and forms a unique and important addition to our poultry literature. Cloth, 12mo. 1.00

The American Standard of Perfection.

The recognized standard work on Poultry in this country, adopted by the American Poultry Association. It contains a complete description of all the recognized varieties of fowls, including turkeys, ducks and geese; gives instructions to judges; glossary of technical terms and nomenclature. It contains 244 pages, handsomely bound in cloth, embellished with title in gold on front cover. $1.00

Stoddard's An Egg Farm.

By H. H. Stoddard. The management of poultry in large numbers, being a series of articles written for the AMERICAN AGRICULTURIST. Illustrated. Cloth. 12mo. .50

www.ingramcontent.com/pod-product-compliance
Lightning Source LLC
Chambersburg PA
CBHW031426230426
43668CB00007B/448